Building a Life

A Mother's Healing Journey of Self-Discovery

JULIE BROWN AND ANGEL LOGAN

BALBOA.
PRESS

A DIVISION OF HAY HOUSE

Balboa Press books may be ordered through booksellers or by contacting:

Balboa Press
A Division of Hay House
1663 Liberty Drive
Bloomington, IN 47403
www.balboapress.com
1 (877) 407-4847

Print information available on the last page.

ISBN: 978-1-5043-8270-0 (sc)
ISBN: 978-1-5043-8269-4 (hc)
ISBN: 978-1-5043-8271-7 (e)

Library of Congress Control Number: 2017909605

Balboa Press rev. date: 09/01/2017

Contents

Preface

When a woman becomes a mother, she becomes a force of nature and a fierce protector of her children. This deep-rooted ability to nurture instinctively develops almost immediately upon the moment she learns of her impending miracle, as everything she knows and believes melds into an infinite tapestry of unconditional love designed to swaddle the tiny life growing within her womb. The capacity to love is so great it is almost impossible to remember life without that feeling.

The dreams that she envisions for herself inevitably fade into one block of sacrifice at a time in order to build a life—a vessel to carry her children into the future. Though this devotion comes with no regret, it can translate into a loss of her identity as she works tirelessly to fill the roles necessary to be the glue that binds her family together, even if that means living without the benefit of her own nurturing. Of course, bookshelves are flooded with "how to" guides offering a myriad of conflicting advice on how to be a good mother. The reality is that motherhood does not arrive with a practical book of instructions; otherwise, no child would ever suffer at the hands of poor parenting. The knowledge that there is no such guide heightens for new mothers the natural fear and uncertainty that come with figuring out how to face and handle the unexpected twists and turns of motherhood.

Building a Life: A Mother's Healing Journey of Self-Discovery is a poignant depiction of how I became a mother before I had the opportunity to discover my own identity. It shows, too, the array of roles I assumed throughout my journey—roles that were thrust upon me by life's unpredictable circumstances.

It's easy to fall into society's preconceived images of what motherhood should portray. I chose instead to devote my life to my family without hesitation, despite my struggle to understand what that life meant. Through a series of challenging and healing experiences, while feeling as though I was blindfolded much of the time, I held onto a small thread of hope; a hope that I would eventually learn how to build a life while embracing all that is special about me.

Foundation of Love

*A **normal day is*** something that we all take for granted; it is the culmination of our routine, daily activities, which range from the mundane to the chaotic. Such days entail going to work, attending school, grocery shopping, and domestic chores. In my case, a typical day finds me standing in the kitchen, preparing a meal.

After one telephone call, that one simple task ceased to exist, as everything that was normal in my life within those few moments had been forever altered. Of course, normal meant something entirely different to me throughout my life, but to hear my daughter utter the words, "Mom, I have a brain tumor," was paralyzing and completely against nature.

In that instant, life as I knew it would never be the same again. How did this happen? How was it even possible? How could I be the mother Jessica needed? Then suddenly, it wasn't the voice of my twenty-seven-year-old daughter that I was hearing at the other end of the phone. Rather, it was the sweet voice of reminiscence—my innocent, little Jessica telling me that she had hurt herself. Only, this time, I couldn't kiss away the hurt and make it feel better. It was the most terrifying and helpless feeling. No mother should ever have to experience it. Parents are not supposed to outlive their children. We are supposed to see them grow to live long, full, and productive lives.

While these thoughts careened through my mind, I wondered how I could avoid the undeniable guilt of making this situation about me.

But then, how could I not? The connection between a mother and child is an inexplicable, bottomless ocean of boundless love wrapped within its own blanket of complexity. A mother wants to absorb any pain that could harm her child. I knew that if I lost my daughter you might as well rip my heart right out of my chest because I didn't know how I could possibly ever breathe again. I stood there within that unfathomable state of panic, clutching the phone in my hand, faced with the horrifying prospect of my daughter's mortality.

It was as though the clock had stopped and had frozen time—only I wasn't there anymore, in that house, on that phone, hearing those words. Instead, I was sixteen years old, standing in a different house with a different phone in my hand. My parents were on the other end of the line as I desperately listened in silence for their reaction, wondering how they would recover from what I had just told them.

Of course, there was nothing normal about that moment either. Now that I think about it, I wonder whether I ever had any normalcy in my life. I guess the only way anyone could answer that question—or how I arrived at this day—would be to understand my unconventional journey and how it all began.

Life had seemed so simple and limitless when I was growing up in Portland, Maine. As far back as I can remember, I think that I could see well beyond the stars within this vast universe. There was a subtle stirring from deep within my soul that had always made me yearn for the unknown world past the walls of my home. I didn't have that in common with my sister, Karen. She was six years younger and always seemed to have more grounded aspirations—somewhat typical of kids growing up in our time. She was the one full of energy, laughter, and corny jokes—always ready to entertain us. My brother, Mark, who was two years older, followed different goals while marching to the beat of his own drum. There were times when I had wondered where he was going to go in his life, but then, I think he had wondered the same thing. I don't think that I could put my finger on any one thing in particular, but I believe there was always something calling out to me that I needed to answer.

I was born in October, 1962, the second child of Karl and Joanne Andersen, who came from Chicago, Illinois. They moved to the East

Coast when my father was in seminary working toward a master's degree in sacred theology. When Mom married Dad, she viewed their new life together as an adventure, and she was brimming with excitement to see where their path would take them. She didn't know about all the pressure that she would face.

During the early years of their marriage, while Dad was in seminary and Mom was at home, she struggled a bit not having him around. She believed in him and wanted Dad to excel in his endeavors, but she missed having all the special moments that most newlyweds shared every day. Back then, it wasn't unusual for husbands to go off for days, weeks, or even months at a time for a job, searching for work or getting the necessary training. The wives generally had to be okay with it. Mom made every effort to be the best wife she could be. But she was lonely. And when Dad did come home, she wasn't as good at doing some domestic chores as she wanted to be, which often discouraged her. She worried that she wouldn't be the kind of wife a minister should expect.

As time progressed, Mom had found herself fighting to meet expectations and fit certain roles. Ultimately, she lost track of her own identity, with little support from family members. This was disheartening for her.

Despite it all, she and Dad worked together as a team with some outside help to overcome her challenges. Amazingly, I never saw that part of their life. By the time I came along and was old enough to be aware of things, Mom had managed to find her way back to herself. My parents' roles had reversed, with Mom becoming the one upon whom Dad relied most of the time. I remember Mom spending her days being the glue that kept our family together and a source of unwavering strength, or so I thought. If she had any doubts or insecurities while I was growing up, she did a fabulous job acting otherwise.

I saw my mother as the pillar of our family—and I think that she had to be to keep us in line. Dad, meanwhile, took all the steps required for him to become a minister. Mom was never easily rattled in front of us. She always had her own quiet distinction, allowing life to unfold naturally without deeming it necessary to control every aspect of every experience. While she may have been climbing a few mountains of her own, Mom was there when we needed her and knew precisely when to step back to give us room to grow. Dad, on the other hand, had a difficult time relaxing. He was a go-getter and needed to be actively doing something most of the time, whether he was working or lending a helping hand. I think that men of his generation felt that they needed to fill their hours with some type of productivity to be the true backbones of their domains. Plus, he loved people and always wanted to help when he could.

His outside activities didn't stop him from keeping his thumb firmly on the pulse of his own family. He always was acutely aware of what was happening within our household. Perhaps being a man of the cloth led him to be more particular when it came to his children. Or maybe he was just a dad who wanted to protect us from the dark elements of the world. Either way, he hovered over us while gently guiding us in the best direction that he could.

Dad was a soft-spoken foundation of virtue, and he walked his walk within the eyes of the Lord. Being a minister was undoubtedly his calling, and that path set the tone for our family. Though our life wasn't inundated with daily scripture readings and threats of brimstone and fire, we still had a clear moral code to follow in a home that was filled with life, love, and laughter. Attending church every Sunday was a regular part of our existence, and, initially, it never occurred to me to question the customary teachings of organized religion; these ways simply shaped how we did things within our family. However, our parents told us that, after becoming confirmed, we were all free to make our own choices regarding faith. Until then, we observed the belief system that they taught us without objection.

Sunday was a big day for us. It began with the church service, followed by socializing with friends from our community and then by a large, early-afternoon dinner at home. We sat around the table catching up on everything that had happened during the previous week, and we ate a meal that was fit for a king. My mother's cooking made it impossible to avoid second helpings, which left each of us stuffed for the remainder of the day. That was fine, because we loved snacking on popcorn later while watching our weekly Sunday favorites together—everything from *Wild Kingdom* to *The Wonderful World of Disney*. This routine might not seem very exciting to anyone else, but it was a regular occasion that I think we all appreciated and will always remember fondly.

There was a time for fun and a time for serious business. My parents had some very strong convictions, beginning with the importance of effective communication. They worked hard to impart them to each of us. It was essential that we learned to express ourselves clearly and deliberately, saying what we needed to say and standing firmly behind our individual viewpoints. We also learned to listen thoughtfully to one another with open minds and hearts. Mutual respect among us was just as vital to our parents because they wanted us to grow into adults with an unbreakable bond tying us together.

I think that one of the most valuable lessons they taught us was about commitment and honoring one's word. They did not want us to start things that we were not willing to finish. If we said that we were going to participate in a project, they expected us to see it through to its completion. If we made promises, we had to keep them, whether it was something big or small. They felt that, if we could honor minor commitments, then we would be able to handle bigger and more significant responsibilities when the time came.

While we understood that money was a must for survival, we also learned how to enjoy life without being driven by it or by the glimmer of material possessions. We liked nice clothes and toys just like other kids, but we learned how to appreciate what we had without feeling like we were missing out if we didn't have the latest and the greatest. Mom had a great gift of showing us how to stretch a dollar into so much more when finances were tight. She could turn a simple meal into a feast and hand-me-downs into high fashion. Even when we didn't have a lot of the extras, vacations were never sacrificed and were always met with great anticipation, endless excitement, and an array of intricate plans.

Mom could turn an ordinary road trip into a spectacular adventure with what we had in the house. We didn't need to spend a ton of money going to restaurants because we packed yummy picnic lunches that she put together and we found that to be so much more fun. Although our early years of traveling didn't include any exotic locations, it was still wonderful seeing different areas of the United States while spending time with many of our extended relatives, including both sets of our grandparents—Gramma and Grampa Valente on my mother's side and Gramma and Grampa Andersen on my father's side.

With both families being from Chicago, the Christmas season was extra special. In my early years, we traveled to Illinois to spend the holidays with them. Christmas day was a celebration like no other, with music, singing, laughter, and a bunch of excited, happy people talking at the same time. Visitors came and went, the kids were playing, and it was the event of the year.

It was never about the number of gifts beneath the tree for our family; it was more about the quality time we had together and the warm and fuzzy moments of the holidays. Our parents didn't go crazy buying presents that they couldn't afford. Instead, they gave us just a few things and taught us the value of one another and how important it was to be together as a family.

Oddly, both sets of grandparents eventually moved from the Chicago area. The Valentes chose to come our way to be near us in Maine, which was great, because we could see them more often. They eventually retired to Florida. The Andersens went in the opposite direction, choosing the state of Wisconsin to be their new home. It would have been nice if they could have moved closer to us, but they provided us with a new and interesting place to visit.

As tightly bound as we were, we never allowed the miles that separated many of us to break our strong connection. Between visits and long-distance telephone calls, we were a family of avid writers, sending letters back and forth frequently through the mail to fill each other in on all of the latest happenings. It didn't matter if someone was writing to announce a major milestone or just writing to say hello. I don't think that I knew too many families who wrote with the enthusiasm and frequency that we did.

I was little when Gramma and Grampa Valente moved to Maine, and I was thrilled. I'd always had an extra special relationship with them. Grampa Valente was full of life and loved to share a million stories with us about his time in Italy when he was a boy, when he moved to the states, and when he became a man and found the woman of his dreams. His stories kept me riveted, eagerly waiting to hear what happened next. I think he was just as happy to tell the stories as I was to hear them.

Grampa Valente (Dominick) was from a small village in Cesuna, Italy, and immigrated to the United States when he was only five years old. He was proud of his Italian heritage, but he was also proud to be an American, and he cherished family more than anything. When he lived in Chicago, while my mother was growing up, he could have taken a higher paying job elsewhere that would have required possible relocation or him being away from everyone for long periods, but making his wife and family happy was his first priority. He chose to take on various types of jobs, from working for the public works department to working at Sherwin Williams, because he wanted to do whatever he could to keep everyone together and happy. He and Gramma Valente rented rooms in their house to boarders to supplement their income, which worked out really well for them.

Gramma Valente (Lillian) was of German and Swedish descent. She had a heart of gold, resolute tenacity, and an infinite capacity to love. When I envisioned the perfect mother, it was her. She had her own firm but considerate thoughts about life, love, and family, and I thought that she knew everything there was to know about being a good mom. She was a housewife who made taking care of a family and home look effortless. I always felt that she understood me on a level that many didn't, and she recognized certain facets of me that I hadn't even fully discovered yet.

My mother had an older brother, Uncle Teddy, who died in 1957. He had been in the garage fixing a car with Grampa Valente when he was electrocuted from a spark during a rainstorm. This nearly broke my grandparents in half, especially Grampa Valente, because he had been standing right there as Uncle Teddy died before his very eyes. During those days, other than medical professionals or lifeguards, most people didn't know how to perform CPR, and there wasn't anything that my grandfather could do to save his son. Uncle Teddy's passing was a tragedy that left an indelible mark upon their hearts.

My mother's younger brother, Uncle Rick, came along much later in life when she was already grown. He was bullied as a teenager when living in Chicago and had been beaten severely by a couple of boys in front of Gramma Valente while they were on the street waiting for a bus. She was lucky Uncle Rick's attackers didn't do anything to her, but she felt helpless for not being able to stop them from harming her son. He recovered, but the emotional scars made all of them weary for a while. This prompted their move to Maine.

On my father's side was my grandfather, Lester Soren, and my grandmother, Oca (pronounced O-SAH) Andersen. It should come as no surprise that they were dedicated to their faith, considering Dad's moral compass and how it guided his life choices. They were traditional people for the most part. However, in many ways, they were ahead of their time, choosing to treat each other as partners rather than living within the conventional male and female roles that most couples observed in those days. They believed in maintaining a united front when in the presence of others, especially with their children, while keeping their disagreements at a quiet decibel and behind closed doors.

Both sets of grandparents were religious and went to their respective churches every Sunday. Gramma and Grampa Andersen followed the teachings of the Unitarian Protestant church, while Grampa Valente had been baptized Catholic. The problem was that Gramma Valente was Lutheran, and although most of the people who they knew were Catholic, Gramma Valente wasn't fond of the idea of converting to Catholicism. Grampa Valente adored her and didn't care about all of that, so they married in the Lutheran church. Then to complicate things just a little more, my mother and her brothers were raised Protestant. It was confusing, to say the least, but I guess that the structure of their belief system didn't matter as much as simply believing. I could respect that.

Grampa Andersen's stoic presence was the first thing that most noticed about him. He was a proud man, who came from a long line of staunch Norwegians, carrying his heritage proudly through his name. Professionally, he was a chemical engineer and took his job quite seriously. In fact, he worked at Sherwin Williams at the same time that Grampa Valente worked there, but they were different men from different social circles and never really connected on a personal level. It didn't help that Grampa Andersen wasn't a very approachable individual. But even more, he certainly wasn't the type to express his feelings to most. You would never have seen him bouncing me on his knee or playing hide-and-seek, but I knew he loved me in his own way, and that is all that mattered to me.

On the other hand, Gramma Andersen was a robust woman with a larger-than-life spirit who loved being around people. She was quite an inspirational person, and she didn't have any problem saying how she felt. Gramma was talented and skilled in the nursing field. In fact, she taught nursing and absolutely loved her job. When she saw anyone in need—whether it was a student, a sick patient in the hospital, or someone within her own family—she was the first one to reach out and do whatever she could to help. Gramma Andersen was content with her own life and didn't put much stock in superficial appearances and domestic chores. But she could sew better than any professional, and she taught me how to sew. Not to mention, she was known as the queen of leftovers and could take a variety of random ingredients from the refrigerator and transform them into a meal. We didn't always know what we were eating, but it generally tasted good. And even if it didn't, you were expected to eat the food put in front of you without question. Because Gramma Andersen did all that she could to help others who needed physical or emotional healing, it wasn't surprising that Dad took his cues from her and chose to become a spiritual healer.

Gramma Andersen was also the cornerstone of our family writing chain, which stemmed from her own personal hardship growing up. She was the eldest of five brothers and sisters, who were split up and sent far away from one another during their childhood upon the unforeseen death of their parents. Being separated from her siblings was devastating, and the only way that she could maintain contact with them was to write each of them regularly. It seemed only natural that she would begin the tradition of letter writing in our family. Consequently, when my father went off to college, he did the same, to keep his parents up on all of his school activities and personal events within his life.

When my parents started dating and decided to get married, both sets of their parents were elated. The two families didn't have a strong connection between one another because they didn't really know each other very well, but they were very supportive of the marriage and always got along fabulously during extended family gatherings.

During the first few years of my parents' marriage, when I was not old enough to hold a pen but big enough to climb out of my high chair, I was a spirited two-year-old running around, wearing a diaper or less and reaching for whatever struck my fancy. Mom told me stories of how I had a great affinity for the mysteries hiding behind closed doors, whether I was peeling the labels off the contents within our kitchen cupboards or voyaging out into the neighborhood for my own outdoor adventure. Sometimes, when my mother thought I was sleeping soundly, I had already climbed out of bed and followed her back downstairs without her knowing it. Other times, before everyone had awakened in the morning, I was walking around outside or down the street visiting the people within our vicinity. My poor mother had to go out to search for me every so often, but she usually found me safe, sound, and happy as a clam at a neighbor's house being fed breakfast, entertained, and cared for. The neighbors didn't mind, but I certainly kept my mother on her toes.

While Mom had her hands full chasing me around, Dad finally received his master's degree from Andover Newton in 1964. Everyone was so proud of him, and Gramma and Grampa Andersen came out to the East Coast to see Dad graduate. When all of the festivities were over, my brother and I traveled to their house with Mom to stay for almost a year, while Dad was doing his clinical duties out of state.

Dad had a ton to do during those years and was away a lot of the time. But when he was home, he devoted his attention to his family and gave us as much of his time as he could.

When we were little and Dad was away, he wrote to us often—not just to Mom, but also to Mark and me, before Karen came along. I missed my Dad when he was at school and later when he was doing his clinical work, but his letters always made me feel special and loved. Whenever the mail arrived and there was a letter waiting for me, Mom sat me down to read everything that Dad had to say. He spoke about how busy he was working on different projects, and he described where he was as a big place that had lots of people. I loved hearing his messages to me.

The letters Dad wrote to my brother, Mark, were more detailed, as Mark was older and could understand more than I could. He told my brother about some of the things that he did throughout his day, like helping people to take baths and making beds. He praised Mark for his performance in school and talked about plans for where we would live when he returned home to us.

Of course, Dad wrote the most to Mom, filling her in on everything he was doing in his clinical studies, from the subject of his reading materials to the work he did as a nurse's aide. He told Mom about some of his friends who he dined with and how much he missed his family. It was sweet how he wrote of his affection for Mom, and it was obvious just how much he loved her.

Dad was an affectionate person who dedicated himself to us, just as much as he did to his ministry. In some ways, I think he tried to make up for the times that he had to be away from the family pursuing his degree in earlier years. I noticed this more when I was around nine or ten years old. Dad's relationship, and thus the activities he shared with Mark, was different from his relationship with us girls; Mark was a boy, and he and Dad had many things in common. When it came to Karen and me, Dad made an effort to connect with us on a different level. I got to go out on a regular date night with Daddy on Saturday evenings. A & W Root Beer was where he took me to have dinner, and we used that time to talk about anything and everything. This enabled him to catch up on anything he may have missed going on with me, and it was a great opportunity for us to bond regularly. Dad would ultimately do the same thing with Karen when she got older.

My brother had dealt with some issues from the time he was old enough to go to school. He faced some challenges that created tension at home. Karen was the baby and didn't understand most of what was going on, and although I didn't always get it, I felt the need to be the "peacekeeper" in the family. I just wanted everyone to be happy. I always looked for ways to smooth the waters if there was conflict in the air, trying to find a way to put smiles on the faces of my family or whatever I could to make things better in our household. It certainly was not a battleground in our home, but I didn't like it when any issues existed, so I did my best to bring everyone together.

My parents often joked about how independent I was, practically raising myself. Even back when Mom was pregnant with Karen, I wanted to help in the house as much as I could. I washed dishes, made beds, and did anything I could find to do that would make things easier for Mom. I liked how it felt to be that person within the family. Even more, I liked the positive attention I received when I did these things.

After Karen was born, I couldn't help but be protective of her. I was so proud to have a little sister. I loved playing with her, getting her dressed in the morning, and taking her everywhere with me. She was my baby doll and I felt like a little mother caring for her. It seemed like a natural role for me.

Because I was so headstrong, it didn't always occur to me that I should let my mother know what I was doing or where I was taking Karen. In fact, one summer, during a visit to Massachusetts while Dad was still in school, I remember getting Karen up one morning while my mother was still sleeping. I dressed her and took her down the street visiting. I'd made a friend that summer, and I took Karen to visit my friend so my mother could sleep longer. It wasn't just that I was taking care of my sister. I wanted to do my very best to care for everyone in my family. Of course, I was only eight years old, going on thirty at the time.

My mother had a few passions, including her interest in nursing and fashion designing. She got married at age twenty-one and started a family right away. That's the way things were done in those days. It wasn't until Karen was about three or four that Mom decided to go back to school to get her degree in nursing. Although she had designed her own wedding dress and had the talent to be in fashion, that dream wasn't as practical as nursing and never came to life.

As I started getting older and eventually reached my teen years, I didn't feel as attached to the role of mothering Karen as I had when I was younger. I was starting to feel smothered when she was always underfoot, which made me pull away from her. I loved Karen dearly, but my independence was beginning to evolve, and I wanted to spend time with my brother and his friends. I was somewhat of a tomboy, and I liked hanging out with the guys. When I least expected it, though, I suddenly started to see them under a different light. And then my world began to change.

Tethered to Uncertainty

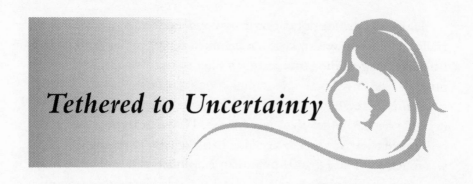

When I was thirteen, I came down with mono, which was widely known as the kissing disease. Of course, that was not the only way to get it. Girls my age never really thought about catching germs from drinking out of each other's cups, using the same spoon to eat some ice cream, or sharing lip gloss. However, those were the most popular ways to spread mono, and once you had it, you were usually down for weeks. I was no exception. I was sick for quite a while and had to stay home for part of the school year until I wasn't contagious anymore.

Around that time in 1976, my brother's friend, Floyd Brown, became interested in me. I wasn't aware of it until my brother told me that Floyd liked me and wanted to go out. Floyd had always been around over the years because he and Mark were tight growing up. Lately, though, he had been hanging out at the house a lot more because Mom and Dad needed some remodeling done to our attic and paid Floyd to do the work. He was really good at building things, and they trusted him to do a good job.

I was still stuck at home recovering. I didn't feel bad, but the doctor expected me to stay home until there was no doubt that the mono was gone. I was used to seeing Floyd at the house with Mark, and while he was working on the attic. I didn't mind chatting with him occasionally to pass the time. Once in a while I made him something to eat, like a sandwich. After all, he was working really hard to do a good job for my parents.

However, the idea of dating Floyd seemed strange to me. I didn't really see him that way, maybe because he was my brother's friend. Still, I liked talking to him, and after a while, our chats became a regular thing.

Somewhere along the line, I began thinking of Floyd as one of my own friends rather than just Mark's. He was easy to talk to, and he listened to what I had to say. It didn't take long to realize that there was much more to Floyd Brown than I had originally thought. Floyd was always a big guy physically, and he exuded a tough, standoffish demeanor. But after spending a significant amount of time with him, I discovered that he was nothing like that at all. He had a gentle spirit with a kind heart and liked helping people. The funny thing was that children absolutely adored him, and he had the patience of a saint.

When Floyd finished working on the attic, he and I started spending time together outside of the house—sometimes with each other and sometimes with a group of friends. It was very sweet and innocent, as he was a perfect gentleman. The first time he kissed me was three months after we started seeing each other. He was so tender and only kissed me on the cheek. He had a way of making me feel like I was the only person in the entire world.

Initially, I thought us dating might be awkward, because of Mark's friendship with Floyd, but that didn't seem to be an issue at all. As we continued dating, we spent more time together. Eventually, we were practically inseparable. When I babysat, Floyd came with me, and I joined him whenever he babysat. I liked the way he made me feel, and I loved being with him. Although he was quiet with most people, Floyd didn't seem to have a problem sharing his personal thoughts with me, and we talked about so many different things.

Floyd was creative and had a passion for building things. It was more than just putting materials together; it was a meticulous and artistic way of transforming the mundane into something beautiful. He did an incredible job on the attic in my house, and I knew that this was only the beginning—that he would do his work on a much larger scale one day.

My mom wrote me this letter on my fourteenth birthday (October 1976):

Dear Julie,

I am writing this letter for two reasons. One, because you are my daughter and sometimes it's hard for me to speak to you without feeling you're brushing me off because I'm your mother. Secondly, because you are about to become 14 years old and there are some things I want to tell you as a friend and as a mother.

You have always been a real joy to be around, and your father and I are very proud of you. We love you very much. You are very different from Mark and Karen and very special in your own way. I have always tried to respect those differences and treat you as an individual. I wouldn't want you to be like Mark or Karen, and I wouldn't want them to be like you. I only want each of my children to be the best of who they are.

Now that you are becoming a young woman, there will be many times when you will want to be alone and do things your own way. You won't want my advice, and you won't want to ask your father or I what to do. That's the way it should be if you are going to grow up to be a responsible, independent person. However, you will also have to take the consequences for your decisions. Your father and I want to be around to love and help you through the times when your decisions or choices don't always work out the way you would like them to, but we know we cannot protect you from being hurt.

You are a sensitive person and get hurt easily, and that's not bad; it is just the way you are. You have a boyfriend now, and as time goes on, you will find times when that relationship is going to cause you to have a lot of different feelings. One minute, you may be so happy you will feel like jumping for joy. The next minute, something may happen and you will feel like it is the end of the world. I do not have much advice about how to handle that, except to say everything passes in time. But I can say that there are a few things you can do to make it a little easier on yourself. One is to not hold on too tightly. People need to be loved and feel loved, but they can't stand to be smothered or made to feel tied down. You need to give people room to grow, and when you try to possess them or get upset when they don't spend all of their time with you, they soon feel cramped and begin looking around for a new place to grow. If you have a relationship with someone, you have to trust it. The relationship you have with Floyd is a good one, I think. But, then again, it might not last.

The second thing I wanted to tell you concerns marriage. I believe in it, and I wouldn't want my life any other way, but I'm sure a lot of my ideas are because of the time in which I grew up. There was very little else for a woman but marriage and children. So, for me, there was no other choice worth pursuing. The future is wide open for you and your generation. You can do most anything you want to do. I am just beginning to discover all the things in life I want to do and what my talents are. You have a chance to discover that early in your life. I am lucky enough to have someone like your father who wants me to be a complete person. A lot of women of my generation were not as lucky as me. Their husbands were perplexed and threatened by their wanting to grow, and their marriages ended in divorce.

If I can offer any advice at all about marriage, it is to say be sure that you are open to growing and that you want the other person to grow too. That's the only way it can work. Many young people today are deciding not to get married or not to have children if they do get married. That is a real choice you have for the future. Look at all the choices you have and consider each of them carefully before you make your decisions. When you do choose, have no regrets. To love one man throughout your life and raise children together can be a wonderful and joyful experience. But it is not the only way to share your life. If you choose marriage, you owe it to yourself and the person you love to find out all you can about marriage. Don't just let it happen and then hope it will work out—search together for a meaning in your relationship. Prepare yourself for marriage … Read and study about different types of marriages and decide what kind of marriage you want together. Then work to make that goal a reality.

Well, I've rambled on enough and I didn't intend to make this a "sermon." I should leave that to your father. I love you so much I wanted you to know me better as a person, and I want to know you better. It's only natural that I should want to share with you what has worked for me and my marriage. I can't speak from the point of view of one who never married because I have not experienced that, but I have read and studied and feel sure now that I have made the right choice for my life. It's a good feeling to have no regrets. I hope someday you'll be able to look back on your life and say the same.

All my love,
Mom

I loved every minute of my time with Floyd, but as time progressed and he became a senior, I worried that dating a freshman wouldn't be enough for him. I didn't want to be the one to hold Floyd back from his future. I guess it made sense in my head at the time, so I broke it off with him. Neither of us had really been with anyone else, so this was a good opportunity for me to date other people, to see what it was like. I don't think Floyd was ever on board with my decision, but he let me do what I needed to do.

I wish I could say that I behaved appropriately, but the truth is that I went a little crazy and started partying. I snuck around and did things that I wasn't necessarily proud of, but I somehow managed to keep from getting caught by my parents. The amazing thing was that, even though I had broken it off, Floyd discreetly hung around and remained in the background, keeping his eye on me and what I was doing. Whenever I got in over my head, he appeared like a knight in shining armor, ready to swoop me up and save me, from myself mostly. My parents were never the wiser and simply thought that, if I was with Floyd, I was fine. He was great about bringing me home—never alerting them to anything. I began to wonder why I'd thought that breaking up with

Floyd was a good idea. He had my back and showed up when I needed him most.

It didn't take much to figure out that Floyd was always going to be in my corner, and perhaps that meant that maybe I was enough. I didn't see any reason to torture myself or him any longer. He was the one I wanted to be with, and I finally saw that he wanted to be with me too.

At the end of the school year, in 1978, Mark and Floyd both graduated. Throughout the summer, we were all busy doing our own thing—I had a job, Mark had enlisted in the service and was scheduled to leave in September, and Dad was traveling here and there going on interviews. We were all living our lives and keeping ourselves occupied. I guess I never put much thought into the out-of-state interviews; I presumed Dad was just trying to get his feet wet with these meetings but ultimately planned to get a position close to home. I didn't understand that he was feeling uncertain about his future in the position he held in the church.

One trip that Dad took was to Florida where my grandparents had retired. This was great because he could combine business and pleasure with a visit to Gramma and Grampa Valente. They loved Dad, and they were happy that he took some time to spend with them.

Imagine my surprise when Dad returned home from Florida having made the decision to accept a position offered to him by the Sarasota Memorial Hospital as the head of the chaplaincy department. I hadn't thought that these interviews were serious or that he would even consider relocation. This was the last news I expected to hear and the last thing in the world that I wanted. How could he expect to uproot us? How could he expect me to leave my school and my friends? I was only a sophomore in high school at the height of my teenage years. Not to mention, this had always been our home, as far back as I could remember.

I felt as though the world was falling apart when he sprung this jolting announcement upon us. My whole life was in Maine. I had a job working at a fabric store, I had friends, I had school to finish, and I had a boyfriend. By that time, Floyd and I had been together for two and a half years; there was no way I would be willing to leave Floyd to move to Florida. What floored me the most was that there wasn't any discussion. It wasn't like Dad was offered the job and came home to ask us what we thought about such a major move. I'm sure the hospital had to know that he was married with children, so it wouldn't have been unreasonable to allow him a few days to talk about it with his family before giving the hospital an answer. However, that did not happen. My parents made this huge decision without even considering the rest of the family. To make matters worse, the move was going to happen in the middle of the school year during the holidays.

To say that I was unhappy was an understatement, and I made my feelings known to everyone. I perceived this decision as very personal for me. I complained, cried, and moped, trying to wish away what I thought was an awful nightmare. I suppose most people would have said that I was being selfish and immature about the circumstances, considering that this was my father's career. It's true—Dad worked hard and sacrificed a lot so he could get the job of his dreams, and that should have taken precedence over the desires of a dramatic teenager. But I couldn't see it that way at the time. I had reached an age where I was doing more things on my own, and I didn't like feeling out of control or the idea that decisions for my future had been taken completely out of my hands.

The move didn't really affect Mark that much. Because of his enlistment, he wasn't going to be around. And Karen was young enough that she wouldn't have any problems adapting to new surroundings, new friends, and a new school. It seemed that I was the only one who had an issue with the move.

Mom knew how I felt and wanted to be sensitive to my feelings. She tried her best to come up with an answer that would make the most sense for the entire family. Eventually, she came up with a solution. Mom suggested that I stay in Maine with a family friend so I could finish high school here with my friends.

While that was a great idea, it still meant that I would be away from my family. Mom wanted to be fair to me, so she left the decision completely within my hands—either I could go to Florida with the family or I could stay in Maine. I wish I could say that the decision was simple because I didn't want to move, but the whole thing was complicated and overwhelming. My ideal solution would have been for Dad to turn down the job in Florida and find one in Maine, so we could all be together without anyone having to move. Mom's suggestion meant that they were definitely moving to Florida, with or without me. She tried to make the situation easy for me by giving me the choice, and I wanted to rise to the occasion—to be the adult who could make this very important decision. However, it just made me physically sick trying to figure out whether I should stay without my family or go with them to start a brand-new life.

Mom saw how this dilemma was tearing me apart and realized that it was too much for me. She finally said, "You cannot make this decision on your own, so I'm going to make it for you."

Mom told me that I would stay only long enough to finish the semester, and then I would have to move to Florida in January to join the rest of the family at our new home. In some ways, I felt relieved that she ultimately took the burden of having to choose away from me, as I wasn't ready to make such an adult decision. However, it still meant that I would be moving away, and I couldn't possibly be happy about that.

Floyd and I hated the idea of being apart. Although a long-distance relationship would be challenging, we were willing to do whatever we could to keep from losing each other. We promised to write, call, and visit as much as we could on vacations, weekends, and any other opportunities. In the back of my mind, I hoped that maybe Floyd would be willing to move to Florida if it was feasible.

My father started to worry that I was trying to prove that I could handle this move while maintaining my relationship with Floyd and that maybe I was getting way ahead of myself, thinking that I could make everything work. I can't say that he was wrong; I definitely felt the need to prove myself, and I had no intention of failing.

The next couple of months flew by like a whirlwind. Mark left for the service. Mom and Dad had their hands full packing for their move, and I had my own "to-do" list; from telling my friends to notifying the school that I would be leaving. It was a lot for me to process. I was beyond stressed and worried about how my relationship with Floyd would withstand the distance. I was not willing to give up on us.

It was 1979, and my parents had made their way down to Florida. I was still in Maine tying up the loose ends of my own life while trying to spend every minute that I could with Floyd. Then, one day in January before I left Maine for Florida, I received some unexpected news that would change all of our lives. To make matters worse, I had to call my parents in Florida to notify them.

I could barely breathe, but no one could call them about this but me. As I uttered the words, I still couldn't believe what I was saying to them. "I'm pregnant."

I just didn't understand how this had happened. Floyd and I had been extremely responsible, and we'd used protection. Sure, people always say that protection is not foolproof, but we were so careful—evidently, not careful enough. I had gone to Planned Parenthood and taken a pregnancy test which confirmed what I already knew deep down inside. I will never forget how judgmental the woman who gave me the results was as she questioned me with her biting tone of condemnation. Instead of being kind and supportive, she immediately interrogated me about what I was going to do, as if I had all of the answers a whole minute after finding out that I was pregnant. Then, she started spouting all kinds of statistics to me about the likelihood of girls my age being able to finish school or last in a marriage. It was surreal to find out that I was definitely pregnant, and listening to some random stranger treating me with such insensitivity wasn't helping me at all. I couldn't take it anymore and I indignantly snapped at her, "I don't plan to be one of those statistics!"

My parents didn't scream and yell, but I knew they were extremely disappointed in me and about my situation. I had rarely experienced their disappointment, and it didn't feel good knowing that they probably thought less of me after we hung up.

There were many things to discuss. In the following days and weeks we spoke frequently over the phone and wrote several letters, as our family always had. Mom was adamant that she wanted me to stick with the original plan to move to Florida that month, but my pregnancy changed everything. It wasn't just about me or my family anymore. Floyd was the father of my baby, and I had to consider what he wanted.

I'm sure my situation broke my mother's heart on a few levels. For one, we usually talked about everything, but when I'd decided that I was ready to have sex, I hadn't talked to her. My mother was blindsided by the news that her teenage daughter was having a baby, especially because she didn't have any clue that I was already sexually active. I didn't keep it from Mom intentionally. It was just that between my dad's new job, their move to Florida, and the direction my relationship was going with Floyd, everything in our lives was happening so quickly. He and I had grown closer, and we took the next step together, not knowing just how that would impact our lives.

The ironic thing was that when I was younger (when someone we knew got pregnant at fifteen and had her baby out of wedlock) I had assured my mother that I would never become a teenage mother. This young mother was a billboard example of all that could go wrong and did. The circumstances in her life were as challenging as you could imagine. The girl was all alone because the baby's father didn't marry her. His family wouldn't allow him to have anything to do with her or the baby. Without the help and support that she needed as a teenage single parent, she had to drop out of school to raise her baby and ended up on public assistance as one of those sad statistics the woman at Planned Parenthood had spouted at me.

Until Floyd and I figured out what we were going to do, I didn't tell anyone about the baby—not my friends at school or at work. There were so many things to figure out, and we were just kids who had made an adult decision about becoming physical in our relationship. We just didn't know that we would be faced with such adult consequences.

Then, in the midst of my mental anguish, I received a seven-page letter from Dad. It was composed and rational but quite surprising. He assured me that, no matter what, he and Mom loved me, and nothing I did would ever change that. But the tone of the letter was very cold and concise. My father proceeded to spell out all of my options in great detail. He talked about abortion, having the baby and giving it up for adoption, keeping the baby, or getting married right away, describing how he thought that each option would impact my life. I think the most shocking part of his letter was when he shared that he—my dad, the minister—was in favor of me having an abortion. He made it clear that, if I chose to keep the baby or marry, my life would be burdensome and that he and Mom would only be a minimal source of support. I didn't know if he thought that having a baby would ruin my life or if he thought that I just couldn't do it. Either way, the decision wasn't his to make. It was mine. I knew that I could never forget the words that my father wrote to me in that letter.

The guilt I felt was horrible. I was concerned about Dad's reputation as a minister, even though my parents had left Maine and severed ties with the local church community. No matter what I chose to do, people would find out about it, and it might reflect poorly upon my dad. Even though it was apparent what he and Mom wanted for me, I understood just how difficult this situation had to be for them. There were so many things to consider. After reading Dad's letter, I finally knew what would be best for me. Naturally, Floyd and I discussed everything first, because I couldn't make such an important decision about whether to keep the baby or not without him. Although he and I were on the same page, nothing was etched in stone, and we agreed that it was time for me to go to Florida.

Mom and Dad knew that I wanted to keep the baby, but I think they hoped that, once I moved to Florida, I would have to listen to them and make the choice they thought would be best for everyone involved. It was one thing to speak with them about my pregnancy over the telephone and in letters, but seeing them face-to-face was going to be another story.

I needed to finish my semester of school first. Then, after several send-off parties, I said all of my good-byes at school and work. I hated leaving Floyd behind, but we pledged our love to each other and promised to reunite when the time was right. My parents were supposed to pick me up at the airport. When I landed, no one was there to greet me. They were running late because of traffic. I have to admit, for a moment, I thought they were so upset with me that they didn't want to see me after all. I felt abandoned and so alone standing there all by myself in the airport. I wasn't sure what to do next. I was crumbling inside but trying to keep myself calm.

Then I looked up and saw my father approaching. I was so relieved and I immediately burst into tears. Dad cried too. He cried because he was happy to see me, but he also cried because he was worried about me and the uncertainty of my future.

Mom wasted no time after I arrived swooping me off to see two different counselors at appointments that she had already scheduled at Planned Parenthood. I'm pretty sure that she thought the counselors would paint a scary enough picture of what life would look like for me as a teenage mom that I would decide to either choose an abortion or give the baby up for adoption.

However, that is not what happened at all. The first counselor spoke to my mother candidly in front of me and told her that I had a really good head on my shoulders and that I definitely knew what I wanted to do. The counselor also recommended that Mom should let me do it, assuring her that my intentions were to finish school and make every effort to have as normal of a life as possible. That was hard for my mother to hear the first time, but it was even harder the second time when the other counselor said basically the same thing.

I was deeply grateful that the counselors supported my decision. Even though I knew I wasn't going to change my mind, I still needed some validation and someone to be supportive of my life plan. Floyd and I had already decided before I left Maine that we were going to keep the baby and get married as soon as possible, but I felt like I owed it to my parents to at least hear them out. Floyd respected that.

Parents have a difficult enough time letting go of their adult children, letting them fly out of the nest and live their lives. My parents had to watch me step into the big shoes of adulthood long before any of us were actually ready.

To make matters worse, I had to tell my eleven-year-old sister that I was pregnant and moving back to Maine to marry Floyd. I needed to explain my situation to her in a way that wouldn't paint a bad picture of me but would discourage her from following my path. This was hard for Karen, who had been waiting and waiting for me to finally join them in Florida. I didn't feel like a very good role model. I felt even worse because we had been very close when she was young, but then, when I became a teenager, I hadn't had as much patience for her. I was just going through typical teenage growing pains, but Karen was too young to understand why I had pulled away from her.

Karen was sad that I would be returning to Maine at some point, but she put on a brave face while I was there and promised that she was happy for me. My parents reluctantly accepted my decision, knowing that the life I had chosen was going to be complicated and riddled with obstacles. I knew it would be hard too, but I felt that it was the best option.

I would never have imagined that I would be having such a profound and pivotal experience in my life as a teenager. Nor had I thought that I would be living 1,500 miles away from my mother when I was to become a mom.

Fortunately, both of my grammas made sure that they kept in touch with me, offering all types of advice and support. Gramma Andersen was quite the seamstress, and I was very grateful that she had taught me how to sew. This was a good skill to have and I was sure it would come in handy at some point. You would have thought that someone her age might have been against marrying young, but Gramma Andersen was amazingly supportive. She believed in me and was sure that I would continue with school and make something of my life beyond being a housewife and mother.

Her modern and independent way of thinking probably stemmed from her earlier tragic experiences, having lost her parents. This experience brought us closer, and while I was pregnant, we talked about a ton of things—from what to expect during pregnancy to what I should do professionally. I thought that I might be interested in some field having to do with animals, but Gramma Andersen insisted that a job in the medical industry, like a medical assistant, would be more suitable and lucrative. Although she meant well, this was what *she* had envisioned for my life; it wasn't really what I had wanted. Still, I thought she knew best, and it made sense to follow her advice. After all, Floyd and I needed to make money if we were going to survive.

I felt many conflicting emotions during this time ranging from excitement to be marrying Floyd and becoming a mother to fear about marrying Floyd and becoming a mother. The hormones and various changes in my body didn't help either. It was just so much to process, and we didn't have the luxury of mulling over things too long. We had to figure out each next step.

On top of everything, Floyd was feeling the weight of his own anguish. His dad was very sick and had been more often than not because of heart complications that stemmed from having had rheumatic fever as a child. Medicine wasn't that advanced when his father was younger, and he eventually ended up suffering through one surgical procedure after the other trying to stay alive. This was difficult on Floyd. It was hard on me too, as his father had always been so nice to me.

When Floyd and I visited his father in the hospital before I went to Florida, I worried that he would be disappointed in us. His reaction was much kinder and more compassionate than I had anticipated and contained no judgment. He shared the story of how Floyd's mother had become pregnant before they were married. This meant a lot to me. I needed to know that there were people who were truly on our side.

I had to give Mom credit. She tried to put her best foot forward while helping me make plans for my wedding to Floyd. I was lonely without him in Florida, but I would be back in Maine soon enough. Life was changing drastically for everyone.

When I returned home, people definitely wondered what was going on and why I was back in Maine without my parents at age sixteen. I didn't have any problems getting my old job back at the fabric store, but I saw the probing looks on the faces of my coworkers, who were trying to figure out what was going on.

It got worse when some of the women found out that I was pregnant. The looks quickly turned from curiosity to contempt as they judged me harshly for my predicament. I was pretty sure that none of the ladies would be hosting a baby shower for me, but I was fine with that. I didn't want people involved in the important aspects of my life if they couldn't be supportive. Maybe I wasn't a poster child for the fair maidens of the world, but I still deserved respect.

I started seeing Dr. Bennert, a friend of my father's, who made sure that I did everything possible to have a healthy pregnancy. He kept my parents updated on my condition with as much information as he could ethically provide which they truly appreciated. From the progression of my pregnancy to my overall outlook, he had good reports to give them about me. I think this helped make my parents feel somewhat better about my future.

Mom encouraged me to plan a small wedding. She didn't want to draw too much attention to my condition. But I wasn't marrying out of obligation. I may have been pregnant and young, but I was still marrying out of love. I didn't plan to marry a second time. I wanted this wedding to be special with everything that I had envisioned for myself. That school of thought, however, came with a price tag. Eight weeks wasn't very long to plan a wedding, but I didn't want to wait and be too far along in the pregnancy on my wedding day. Plus, many of our relatives would be traveling from far away to attend the occasion, which meant we had to expedite everything to make it work.

We planned a spring break wedding on April 14. Without financial support from anyone, Floyd and I paid for just about everything. We both worked as many hours as we could to make sure we had the wedding of our dreams. Mom helped with some of the planning, but she left most of it within my hands. As if we didn't have enough to do, we also had to attend premarital counseling through someone Dad knew.

Floyd and I had to work right up until before the wedding to make sure we had the funds to pay for all of the vendors. We did some serious bargain shopping, managing to keep the cost for the entire wedding, serving a hundred guests at under a thousand dollars. This was miraculous.

My intention was to wear my mother's wedding dress which she and her sister-in-law had both worn. Mom had designed it herself twenty years earlier. It was an elegant gown made of silk with fabric rosettes and a long row of tiny buttons down the back. However, when I tried it on in January, it was snug. I was just barely pregnant and not even showing at that point. I knew I would be bigger by the time the wedding arrived. I was so disappointed, but Floyd's dad did something special to make it better. His gift to me was to pay for the purchase of a new dress, which was beautiful and what I wore instead. Mom saved her dress for Karen to wear one day.

During the hustle and bustle of the wedding plans, Dad was anxious to talk with Floyd. He hadn't seen Floyd since before my parents left

Maine. Dad wanted to talk to my future husband before he allowed me to walk down the aisle. Dad wrote a letter to both of us explaining that he was feeling more comfortable about our choice to marry and have the baby. He talked about looking forward to being a father-in-law and a grandfather. To my surprise, Dad admitted that he was glad I hadn't opted for an abortion. I felt better knowing that Dad's position had changed and that he was really trying.

Although he was willing to give us his blessing and legal permission to marry, he needed more time to be okay with letting me go on an emotional level. This was perfectly understandable considering my age and all that I was about to embark on in my life. Dad was asking for Floyd's patience and understanding while they worked through that together.

Mom and Dad made arrangements with the church. I was lucky enough to have had more than one bridal shower thrown in my honor. That might seem excessive, but it was actually helpful for us, given that we needed just about everything. Neither of us had ever been on our own and we were starting our new life together from scratch.

I was to wear an opal ring that was passed along to me from my grandmother, with matching wedding bands that Floyd and I purchased.

Despite the circumstances surrounding our marriage—from our age to an early pregnancy—this day was special to me. I didn't want to rush through it or minimize our wedding. Our baby had been conceived out of the love that Floyd and I shared. We may have been young, but I was not embarrassed by that or ashamed. Ideally, it would have been better to wait until we were older and more aware of life and ourselves. I had to believe that things happened for a reason and there was a reason that our baby came into existence.

I did my best to savor every moment of our wedding day. Relatives from both sides of the family came from all over to be there for us, and that meant the world to us. Even though Floyd's dad had been through so much with his health from multiple hospital stays to his recent open-heart surgery, he was adamant about attending our wedding. Fortunately, his doctors gave him their approval, and he was able to be with us.

Shortly before the reception, Floyd and I shared a few quiet moments together. It was during that time, as I was absorbing everything from our day, that I realized that I had walked through the portal of adulthood when I said my vows. My age was not going to be a factor any longer. Everything I knew up until then was about to change because I had become a married woman.

Because I had worried about how my friends would treat me when they found out that I was pregnant, I had kept most of them at arm's length. Surprisingly, they were fairly supportive, and most didn't judge me at all. Some of the junior high cheerleaders who I still hung out with gave me a baby shower, which I really appreciated. A handful of my friends came to our wedding. I wish I hadn't felt so closed off from them and most people, but I chose to keep my distance as a defense mechanism for my own self-preservation. I didn't want to feel vulnerable and needy. I just wanted to move on and put my energy and focus into building a life with Floyd and our baby. This meant earning an income, putting a roof over our heads, and learning how to stand on my own two feet.

We stayed in a hotel for our wedding night, and the next day, which happened to be Easter Sunday, we met our family for brunch before they were scheduled to fly out. Later that day, Floyd and I left to travel through New England for our honeymoon. We didn't stay away for the whole week. It was my spring break, and I needed to get back to school—not to mention, I was almost five months pregnant.

When I returned to school, it seemed like I started showing almost overnight. Many of the kids in school didn't notice initially, and the majority remained unaware that I was pregnant. Because I could sew, I enjoyed making a lot of my own clothing, which I designed to be a baggier style than the form-fitting store bought clothes that I used to wear. I'm sure it was a surprising fashion statement, but it helped to hide the areas of my body that were growing so quickly and keep the attention off of me for a while.

I needed to earn an income while I was in school, and sewing seemed like the logical solution. I did some sewing for a few of my teachers and some of their friends, but I knew that they were starting to wonder why I needed the money so badly.

Then, one teacher caught me off guard and said, "Julie, I saw your wedding announcement in the Sunday paper."

I said, "Yep, that was me."

I guess the cat was out of the bag—at least with the teachers. I didn't think it would be very long before most of the students found out too. So I decided to take control of the situation. When I had an English paper to write, I wrote about planning a wedding based on my own experience. It was an easy topic, and I had plenty of knowledge in that area. I was surprised to discover that many still didn't realize that the paper was about my own wedding planning experience.

I managed to get through the school year with very few issues, and teachers were very understanding and helpful to me when I needed it. My pregnancy was fairly smooth with the exception of one day that I had to miss. This was mortifying because Floyd had to be the one who wrote the note to excuse me from school. He was my husband and the legal adult figure in my life as I was still under age. Needless to say, after that, I did everything I could to make sure I didn't miss any additional days of school to avoid that embarrassment. I made the best of my situation, finished my school year with honors, and received an award from the National Honor Society. I was proud of myself.

Floyd and I were caught between two different worlds. After all, we were really just kids when we started our life together. In many ways, we were forced to grow up almost immediately in order to assume the adult roles of spouses and parents. But in other ways, our growth had been stunted, because we didn't experience the natural evolution of life and learning. We were so inundated by the daily chronicles of living and surviving—paying bills, putting food on the table, finding work, and being parents—that we didn't develop mentally or emotionally in the way most do. We had to settle into our new roles without really knowing ourselves or each other. Floyd and I didn't have the chance to grow as a couple and build our love the conventional way. Because our existence was tethered to our immediate needs, we had to figure out what it meant to create a home, how to generate income, and how to be a family instantly.

While we were attempting to be grown-ups, the truth was that we couldn't afford to live on our own initially. Floyd's parents let us live with them for a couple of months until we were able to get on our feet and find an apartment of our own. I'm sure my parents appreciated that the Browns were there for us. Both sets of parents got along, though Floyd's father seemed to be a little less comfortable around my dad during my pregnancy. I wasn't sure whether or not it was just a religious thing, but Floyd's parents were in our corner and extremely supportive of us as a couple.

When we finally moved into our apartment, one obstacle after the other jumped into our path. Making a go of it was not easy for us. Money was tight, and we were living in a grown-up world with grown-up responsibilities. We had a ton of bills, from our living expenses to my pregnancy care. Fortunately, we had stored all of our wedding gifts in a closet at my in-law's house until it was time to move, which provided us with many needed household items.

Healthcare wasn't cheap. We couldn't swing everything alone, and I wasn't sure how far into my pregnancy I would be able to work. So I applied for state assistance to help us temporarily. I thought that the system would help a couple like us, who were taking responsibility, working hard, going to school, and trying to build a good life for our family, rather than giving up or becoming a statistic.

However, no one really cared about all of that. We were just another couple looking for a handout, and the mere nineteen dollars per month in food stamps that the state agencies gave us was barely enough to feed a pet, never mind a family of three.

I was extremely thankful that, included in the weekly letter Gramma Andersen mailed to me from the day she found out I was pregnant, was five dollars. In addition to being comforted by her words, I appreciated the extra money. If for any reason she didn't send it one week, she sent double the following week. To some, five dollars might not be a lot, but it sure came in handy for us. I did my best to make it stretch out for whatever we needed, whether it was to pay for my school lunches, baby supplies, or gasoline for Floyd.

Every day was a grind, filled with strife and endless worry. I felt stressed and overwhelmed by the pressure of trying to survive. I had no doubts about Floyd's or my desire to have a life and a family together, but I was still a kid and wasn't fully prepared for everything we had to handle. I missed sleeping in my own bedroom in my parent's house, having my personal possessions that belonged only to me, and having the freedom to live without the concern of paying utility bills and rent. Suddenly, I was living this life where everything I had didn't belong to *me* anymore; we shared everything.

I wrote my parents a letter explaining how I was feeling. But also, I wanted them to know that, despite the challenges—and there were many—I had no regrets and I was determined to make it work, no matter what. There were so many things about my childhood that I missed, especially just being with my family, but I was part of something new and wonderful – my own family. Knowing that and knowing the love that Floyd and I felt for one another, I could get through anything.

Floyd was very sweet to me throughout the pregnancy, trying to make sure that I had everything I needed. He went to Lamaze class with me, and that helped me to feel more secure about what would happen during childbirth. I have to admit that I was nervous about the whole thing, but the Lamaze instructor made it sound so normal and effortless. After all, women had been giving birth to babies since the beginning of time. But I was still just a teenager, and the idea was scary.

During the summer, I spent some time with Floyd's family at their camp, which was a good atmosphere for me, while Floyd commuted back and forth for work. Everything that Gramma Andersen taught me about sewing was extremely helpful, as I continued to create outfits for myself and other people. Gramma Andersen wrote to Mom and told her that she was proud of me for all that I was doing and for keeping a nice apartment. That type of validation helped to keep me motivated.

Before I knew it, we were upon the due date near the end of August, but my baby clearly wasn't ready to arrive yet. Mom, Karen, and Gramma Valente were already here with me, but I didn't actually go into labor until September 1, the day before they were all scheduled to go back home. The hospital staff closely monitored me, because delivering a baby at an age when my own body hadn't fully developed yet was considered high risk. They didn't want to take any chances.

Everything I had ever heard about the pain of childbirth was true. It physically hurt beyond belief. But also, it was an indescribable and profound experience seeing this tiny new life that had been living within me for most of the year enter into this world as his own little person. After twelve hours of labor, our son, Jeremy Joseph Brown, was born at 4:28 a.m. He was healthy and strong, weighing in at eight pounds, two ounces.

I needed my mom to be there with me, and I was so thankful that she didn't go home. She arranged to stay with me for the entire week after I got home from the hospital. Mom was such a huge help to me, but she handled everything in a very respectful and delicate manner, trusting me to make my own decisions and only offering advice when I asked. Those were days of growth for me as I navigated through the first defining moments of being a mother.

Yielding to Expectation

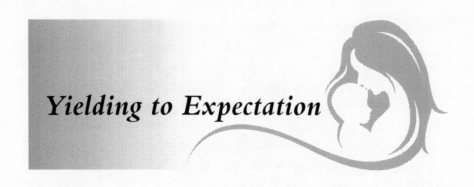

I quickly learned that time didn't stop and the world didn't wait for me to become a mother. I was just one small person in a gigantic universe of mothers and babies, figuring it all out just like everyone else. The most pressing matter was finding a babysitter for Jeremy. I had assured the counselors that Mom took me to, as well as my parents, that I would not let school fall by the wayside, and I intended to keep that promise.

Before Jeremy was born, I managed to find a wonderful woman who I scheduled to take care of him during the morning hours once I began attending my classes. It was amazing that I gave birth to Jeremy and had started the semester one week later, only missing three days of school. Because I was still nursing, I had to pump enough milk every night to fill a bottle to leave with the sitter when I dropped him off on the way to school every morning. Then, every day after lunch, I left school early to pick up Jeremy from the sitter. I took him home, nursed him, and then grabbed a quick nap while he slept. Sleep was a hot commodity. I had to rest whenever the moment presented itself. This was a daunting schedule and breastfeeding took a lot out of me. I wanted to nurse Jeremy longer, but because I was so exhausted trying to balance motherhood with being a student, I could only do it for six weeks; I was still stuck between two worlds.

Our budget was practically nonexistent, and after we paid our bills, we weren't left with enough money for food. I skipped meals more often than not, to make sure that Jeremy could eat regularly. Once he was on whole food, we were able to get a small charge account at a nearby corner store where we could buy his baby food, but Floyd and I barely ate. Thank God the Browns always had a big Sunday dinner, because we had one substantial meal that we could count on weekly to sustain us. Our way of doing things wasn't ideal and it was a struggle, but somehow we made it work and did the best that we could with what we had.

At one point, my father had planned to fly in for a visit. When Floyd's dad realized that we didn't have much food in the house, he gave me a hundred dollars to go to the market for groceries. He didn't want my dad to arrive and find our cupboards bare. I don't think Floyd's dad had even realized how bad it was for us until then. The Browns were very kind and generous. They helped us as much as they could, but they had their own budget to follow and we were trying not to burden them.

When I corresponded with my mother, I tried to clue her in on some of our money troubles without getting too detailed about it. I didn't want to complain too much. But she was smart, and I think she knew that we were having it rough.

Despite all of the challenges we faced, I kept up with my studies in school, and I made the honor roll at the end of the first semester. It gave me a great sense of accomplishment, especially with all that I had to juggle in my life. There were times that I wanted to feel like a normal kid, but I wasn't normal. The other kids my age were living at home with their parents, worrying about high school dances, football games, and who they had a crush on, without a care in the world. I was living the life of an adult.

Even though Floyd was older than me, most of the guys his age weren't trying to support a wife and a baby. They were going to college or just figuring out what they wanted to be when they grew up. I wish Floyd and I had talked about things more often. Maybe it would have helped to know that he was feeling the same way that I was. Instead, we just had a quiet understanding that we would do whatever it took to survive and build the best life possible; we never really discussed any of our problems.

I continued sewing, and I got really good at it. I sewed for as many people as I could to make money, and I did as much sewing for us as I could to save money, making outfits for Jeremy and clothing for both of us. It went well most of the time—until the occasions when I ran out of fabric. That wasn't too much of an issue when I was sewing for customers, but it happened one time when I was making a coat that I really needed. I couldn't finish it until we made enough money to go back to the fabric store for more material. This seemed to be our theme. We would do well for a short time, and then we would fall behind again.

It was wintertime, and Floyd got hired to do some snow plowing. Those jobs usually paid well, but we needed snow for him to plow. We were both desperately wishing for snow that year. Without that money, we wouldn't have made enough to cover our bills and everything else for our Christmas trip to Florida to spend the holidays with my parents. It seemed as though we were always just on the edge of everything, waiting for things to work out in our favor or not, usually with money being the biggest issue.

Christmas was always one of my favorite holidays, and I had the best memories of Christmas in Chicago with the grandparents. I was feeling particularly excited about it this year. Floyd and I may have had our fair share of obstacles, but it was Jeremy's first Christmas and my first one as a wife and a mother. I wanted it to be special, and I knew that it would be, spending the holidays with everyone in Florida. I missed them so much!

True to form, Mother Nature dumped a bunch of snow on New England, especially in Maine, and the snowfall came just in time, as Christmas was right around the corner. We had just enough money to have a nice Christmas in Florida.

When we arrived, I felt the weight of everything at home lift off my shoulders and allowed myself to relax a bit. It was great to see everyone for Christmas. Mark almost didn't make it, which would have been a huge disappointment. However, everything worked out, and Mark arrived on the afternoon of Christmas Eve. It was a good thing, because the other big event that was happening during our trip was Jeremy's christening. We planned to baptize him later that evening. My baby boy was so handsome in his little red velvet suit and bow tie, while my dad beamed with pride to be christening his grandson.

This was the Christmas that I had dreamed of for Jeremy and for us. We took in every moment. We socialized with several relatives from all over the states, who were happily reunited, sharing stories of the past, bursting into endless laughter, and genuinely enjoying each other's company. It was nice to have a break from all of our issues at home without having to worry about whether or not we had enough money to eat. But eventually, we would have to get back to reality.

The holidays were here and gone in the blink of an eye, and we were back in Maine to resume our normal routine. I couldn't help but feel a little nostalgic after being with the family during the holidays. It wasn't that I didn't appreciate Floyd and Jeremy. But a part of me felt sad. I missed seeing my parents, Karen, and Mark on a regular basis. I wanted them to be a part of our lives and to see Jeremy more often than the occasional visit. When Floyd and I got married, my life changed drastically—almost overnight—and I suppose I was still adjusting. Thankfully, we continued to be a family of writers, and our letters traveled from state to state between all of us.

Floyd and I had been married for nine months, and we had an extraordinary son who was growing like a weed. I finally understood why parents often told their kids to stop rushing to be older, as it would be here before you knew it. I finally got it; it was almost painful to see my baby getting bigger so quickly. He was changing and doing something new and different almost every day, outgrowing his outfits before I could buy or sew him new ones, and he was becoming more curious about everything he saw.

Jeremy's growing didn't slow down. Nor did his need for new clothing. The most cost-effective way to keep him dressed was to sew everything. But I ran into a problem when my sewing machine stopped working. It was a vicious cycle. We needed the machine to make money, but I couldn't use it again until I got it repaired, and those repairs would cost us more money. As a child, I never realized that everything in life had a cost, but as a wife and mother, I learned that particular life lesson right out of the gate.

Once I was able to get my machine back up and running, my sewing helped, but I couldn't get enough customers to make a reasonable income. In addition, I got a job working at a fast food restaurant. It wasn't my dream career, but it helped supplement our income. Plus, as an employee, I was provided with a free daily hot meal and a sandwich to bring home to Floyd every night. We didn't worry much about the lack of nutritional value eating burgers and fries all of the time; we were just happy to be eating regularly.

Floyd generally didn't have a problem finding jobs. It was keeping the job that was the issue. He was usually the youngest hired and almost always at the bottom of the totem pole. When layoffs happened or projects dried up, he was usually the first one to be let go. No one ever complained about the quality of his work or his dedication, but there were plenty of guys who had been in the business much longer than him, were older, and almost always had first pick. The situation was frustrating for Floyd, and it wasn't helping our finances one bit.

Then, by sheer luck, he found a long-term job that brought in a steady check. We finally got a break. Floyd liked the work, and his employers seemed to be pleased with his performance. The benefits weren't bad, and he had a chance for advancement, as well as regular raises. The starting salary wasn't that high, but he took whatever carpentry side jobs he could get to make up for the lower pay.

By spring, Jeremy had figured out how to stand up all on his own and walk around while holding onto the edge of his playpen or the furniture in the room to keep from toppling over. He was so cute with such determination on his face. If he fell down, he scrunched up his eyebrows with complete concentration, while he braced his body to get right back up again. I knew that he would be walking on his own before long. I loved watching him grow through each stage as his mind developed and he became more independent. And there was a bittersweet feeling too. I was eager to see who he was becoming, but also, I wanted to keep him as a baby for as long as I could. No one ever said that it would be easy.

Overall, Jeremy was very good most of the time. He had a mild temperament and rarely had big crying fits, even when he was feeling discomfort from teething, needed a diaper change, or was tired. I was extremely lucky with him. His temperament made it easier for me to continue going to school than it might have been, without the worry of my schedule being too hard on him.

Getting my education meant a lot to me, not only for myself, but also for my folks. I didn't want to let them down. My son was too young to understand at the time, but I wanted him to know later on in life that his mother never gave up on her education. I was exhausted most of the time, but my hard work continued to pay off with all of my school achievements. My parents couldn't come up to Maine for the ceremony, but having Floyd in the audience when I was presented with my award made me proud.

By that time, Floyd and I had been married for a year, and we seemed to have found our groove. We didn't have a lot of money for extras, but we were keeping food in our stomachs, paying our rent and monthly bills, and making sure that Jeremy had everything he needed. We created a routine that worked fairly well for us.

Unfortunately, our babysitter got very sick in the month of May, which changed everything. She had been caring for Jeremy from the beginning and was incredible with him, which made it possible for me to go to school and work part-time. I relied on her, and I trusted her implicitly. Even more important, Jeremy responded well to her. I didn't know how I was going to be able to juggle everything without her or find someone else as responsible as her who could take over caring for my son.

Of course, my natural reaction was to call my parents. I was beside myself and cried to my mother, "What are we going to do? I'm going to have to drop out of school or go to night school."

I didn't understand how everything had fallen apart so quickly after we had managed to get ourselves on track. Was this what it meant to be an adult? Or were we having these problems because we weren't old enough or mature enough to cope with everyday living?

My mother listened to me as I sobbed over the phone, and then she made an unexpected suggestion. She proposed that we move down there and let her watch Jeremy while I finished school in Sarasota.

As much as I missed being with my family, I didn't like the idea of moving to Florida for a few reasons. First, Maine had always been my home, and it was the place where I was building my life with Floyd and Jeremy. Also, I didn't want to be a failure. I wanted to make it all work, and I wanted everyone to see that I had made the right decision by choosing this life. Then there was Floyd's family. My in-laws were used to seeing us frequently and spending time with Jeremy. How could I move Floyd and Jeremy so far away from them?

Mom had given us something to think about, and we needed to decide one way or the other right away. I explained what was going on to Floyd's mother and told her about our dilemma. I wanted her to know how much I valued her opinion and how much Floyd and I appreciated having her and her husband as an important part of our lives. She was incredibly supportive, and even though she didn't want to see us go, she told me that we should do what was best for us. I know that my in-laws would have done more if they could, but with Floyd's dad in and out of the hospital, they had more than enough to contend with in their own lives. They couldn't give us the help we needed, and without adequate daycare for Jeremy, I wouldn't have been able to finish school. The bright side was that moving to Florida would temporarily lighten our load, giving us a chance to get back on our feet again and save some money.

I tried one more time to find someone who could take care of Jeremy. The sister of a friend of mine could watch him two mornings a week while she was a stay-at-home mom with her own child. That was pretty much the deciding factor for us. Floyd and I agreed that moving in with my parents would be the only viable solution. However, classes were almost over, and I needed to at least finish that school year in Maine to make transitioning into a new school smoother for my senior year in Florida.

I took Jeremy to the new sitter on the two mornings that she was available, and I brought Jeremy to school with me for the other three mornings only for homeroom attendance. Then I went to each teacher, got my assignments, and went home with Jeremy to do all of my homework. This was not, by any means, the most conventional way of handling things, but I didn't have a choice. My teachers could have been judgmental or taken a hard line with me about it, but they seemed to be willing to work with me and were understanding about my babysitting issues. I think they even respected me a little, as I was working hard and doing everything I could to continue my education.

I couldn't hide the fact that I was a teenage mom with a baby and a husband from the other kids at that point. But honestly, I had neither the time nor the inclination to care. I had to focus on the things that I needed to do for myself and for my family.

Floyd and I had a lot to do to prepare for our move to Florida. We couldn't take everything with us to my parents' house, and we couldn't afford to store it, so we sold all of our furniture and used that money we got to finance our move. It felt as though we were starting all over again. That was really disheartening. We had finally been building something of our own in Maine, and it had all collapsed when we couldn't find adequate childcare for Jeremy. Just one thing had the power to turn our lives upside down. This made me realize just how close to the edge we were living from one day to the other and from one check to the next, hoping that we would survive yet another week. Clearly, we needed the help.

While I was mourning the impending loss of our home in Maine, Floyd was surprisingly enthusiastic about the move—more than I would have thought he'd be. He had never traveled very far for any length of time, other than to Ohio where some of his relatives lived or to Florida to see my family for the holidays. The idea of starting over in a new place was kind of exciting for Floyd, and he was looking forward to embarking on a new adventure. I told myself that, if he could be positive about it, then I could be too.

Before we left Maine, I thought it would be smart to contact the high school in Sarasota ahead of time to arrange my fall enrollment. It was a good thing that I didn't wait until we got to Florida, because transferring schools was more complicated than I thought it would be. My new high school was not as understanding about my status as a mother as my old school in Maine had been. When they saw how much time I had missed during my junior year to care for Jeremy, they said that I had to attend summer school to meet all of their credit requirements before I could be eligible to start as a senior in the fall. This was another setback that I wasn't thrilled about, but if this was what I needed to do, then so be it.

No sooner than we had arrived in Florida, I had to begin my summer classes, which were all in the morning from 8:00 a.m. to noon for three weeks straight. In the grand scheme of things, summer school wasn't going to last that long, and it wasn't going to kill me. Mom and Karen were happy to watch Jeremy while I went to school, and the classes were only in the mornings, which left my afternoons free to be home with Jeremy. The best part was that I didn't have to worry about being bogged down with homework. We did our work during class in these summer sessions. It definitely wasn't as bad as I thought it would be, and as usual, I made it work.

While I was taking my classes and getting us settled in at my parents' house, Floyd was out applying for jobs at various construction sites. But he didn't have any luck finding anything. There were days when he was feeling discouraged, but he wasn't about to give up.

He kept at it until he found out about a position as a carpenter for the hospital. He put in an application, and while he waited for word on that position, he continued looking for other jobs. He had plenty of other things on his list to do too—taking care of necessary errands, getting his Florida driver's license, and signing up for car insurance. His days were filled with things to do, while I continued with my summer classes. I finished with a 95 average, and I was definitely all set to start school in the fall as a senior.

Floyd wanted to do something special for me to celebrate, and he surprised me with a romantic boat ride on the bay. It was good for us to have that time together, because we hadn't had the time or the money for date nights in Maine.

While Floyd was looking for work, he met a guy named Jack, who was also in construction and trying to find the right job opportunity. The two struck up a conversation and hit it off almost immediately. They thought that the combination of their individual skills would be an ideal fit for starting their own construction business, rather than constantly having to pound the pavement for work from companies that would only keep you for a short time. Teaming up as partners would give them more control, and they would be responsible for their own clientele. It had been a tough year for both of us. Seeing Floyd feeling energized by this new endeavor warmed my heart.

The guys wasted no time and jumped right into it. They figured out their overall business model, printed up business cards, purchased the necessary equipment, and started looking for a reliable vehicle with enough space to carry all of their tools and building materials to designate as their company truck. They were off to a great start.

Jack had been living in St. Louis for several years, but he'd recently moved to Florida where his parents resided. He was originally an artist, which made the partnership perfect—Floyd was very artistic about his own work. Between their creative eyes and ambition, it seemed as though this union was meant to be. It was funny watching them devise plans and come up with new ideas. They thought so much alike that they were practically finishing each other's sentences.

They did mostly painting jobs initially, which gave them a good foundation for their business. Jack was great at painting eye-catching signs for their customers. However, very quickly, people got word of how good the duo was, and Floyd and Jack ended up with more jobs than they could handle, from painting to building. They were so swamped with customers that they had to work seven days a week to stay on top of everything. They built a good reputation within a relatively short period of time and gave some of the other construction outfits a run for their money.

The only problem was that Floyd's partner was starting to fall behind and couldn't keep up with the work. They had a system that was effective, but they had to rely on each of them doing his part according to schedule. Otherwise, it would cost the client more money and cost them their credibility.

Floyd wanted to give Jack a chance because he liked him. He didn't want to dissolve their partnership if it wasn't necessary. But no matter how hard Jack tried, he couldn't keep up with Floyd or their customers' projects. It was only a matter of time before Floyd would need to venture out on his own. When they'd started, Floyd had set up everything in his name and made sure that he had all of the required licensing for the business. It wasn't going to be that difficult to make a break if Jack couldn't keep up his end of the deal, which was what happened.

I was glad that Floyd had solid work doing what he loved, which helped us save money, but he was spending more and more time away and less time with Jeremy and me. I know it must have been hard on him not being able to see his son that often, but there had to be a way to create some balance.

Floyd's absence didn't stop Jeremy from taking over the house, as he began walking on his own without needing to hold onto anything.

Once he mastered that, he was up and running from one end of the house to the other, especially if he had an audience. He was quite the little ham, full of smiles and giggles. Jeremy was also a little fish in the water and loved every minute of splashing around the pool when we took him swimming.

I continued to be astounded by my son's sweet evolution—from his distinctive personality to his handsome appearance. He was so much fun to be around and brought joy to everyone in his presence. Living at home with Mom and Dad wasn't always a picnic, but Jeremy had a knack for lightening the atmosphere around him.

It was different for Floyd when we lived with his folks, because he was already a legal adult, and their interaction was different. But when we moved in with my parents, I was still a teenager going to high school while walking in the shoes of an adult as a wife and a mother. Needless to say, it was a complicated dynamic, which made me feel uncomfortable at times as I tried to navigate through my varying roles.

One minute, I had been a daughter under the care of her parents, and just a year later, I was caring for my own child. It made my head swirl. But I was grateful that my parents opened their doors to us during a time when we needed it the most. That break helped us get on our feet and figure out what to do next. A few awkward moments were not going to be the end of the world.

As I spent more time with my mother, I noticed that she was transforming before my eyes into a different and more independent woman. Over the summer, she started working in a doctor's office a few times a week and then began taking a creative writing course. I guess I couldn't be surprised by that, considering the number of letters she had written over the years. I have to say that it did my heart good to see Mom doing something to nurture her own spirit. She took care of Dad, she took care of us, and she was finally doing something to take care of herself. I liked it.

September arrived, and so did my senior year of high school. I liked the idea of being the new student who no one knew anything about; I had a chance to be as normal as I could be. I wasn't necessarily trying to hide that I was married with a child, and I never took off my wedding ring, but I wasn't waving a flag announcing the personal details of my life either. If someone specifically asked me something, I would answer. Otherwise, I kept my private life private.

Floyd drove me to school every morning and put my bike in the back of his truck to drop off with me. Then, when school was out in the afternoon, I rode my bike home, which oddly made me feel like a normal teenager.

My life was so different from anything I could have ever imagined, but being in the house with my family and spending time with my sister made it feel like the old days. When I'd gotten married and chosen to build my life in Maine with Floyd, my sister had struggled with it. Our time together in Florida was healing for both of us.

When Mark was discharged from the service, he came home too. What a reunion! My parents had all of us under the same roof again, along with a few additions—Floyd and Jeremy. Floyd was stoked to have his friend back. Although he was pretty flexible about most situations with little complaint, he'd had to uproot his life by choosing to move to Florida, away from his family and friends. I think being able to hang out with Mark again and do things together the way they had when they were younger really helped make Floyd feel more at home. The house was bustling with people, but somehow, we all managed to make it work with our various schedules and activities.

While everyone else was consumed with whatever he or she was doing, I was dealing with a few personal issues. I was starting to question aspects of myself. I didn't feel very good about my physical appearance or my growing displeasure with the monotony of school. I didn't have any difficulty getting high grades. In fact, everything came so naturally that I didn't feel challenged at all, which made school a boring experience for me.

I spoke with my English teacher, who wasn't surprised by what I was feeling and told me that I was "too smart." I hadn't thought of it that way, but whether the work was too simple or I was too smart didn't matter. I needed to find a solution to the problem. I had always done well in school, but I suppose my way of thinking had changed, along with my level of discipline since I had become a wife and a mom. Most kids my age were focusing on their plans for college but generally didn't have any real responsibilities. I, on the other hand, had to think like an adult, and that heightened my commitment to school. Not doing well just wasn't an option.

In an attempt to find a way to make school more interesting and beneficial to me, I contacted the vocational school in our area about starting classes after I graduated. I thought that targeting my coursework toward a medical assistant curriculum would transition me into an actual career within a reasonable timeframe. I had to go through an application and an interview process, but this would put me in line for an internship later and a job at some point. I was beginning to feel as though I had some achievable career options, which would result in a decent income.

After figuring out my issues with school, I realized that the remaining superficial facets of my life could be easily addressed, by making the choice to do something about my problems rather than wallowing in them. I just needed a new haircut, a better diet, and more exercise—simple changes that would be good for me.

With a more concrete plan in the making, I was able to focus on the approaching holidays. I wanted to give Floyd a gift that he would appreciate more than a plain old pair of socks or a shirt. Then I came up with the idea to have photos taken of Jeremy and me. Floyd worked a ton of hours, which made it possible for me to plan everything without him knowing what we were doing. The pictures came out wonderful, and I knew that Floyd would be happy with his gift.

Living with my parents meant they were able to see us every day, but my in-laws hadn't seen us in quite a while. Floyd and I thought it would be a good idea to spend Christmas in Maine with his family. We left the week before Christmas with Jeremy, and we took Mark with us. Flying would have been too expensive, but with three people to share the driving duties, we were able make the trip in good time and save a few dollars.

My parents didn't outwardly object to our plans, but this was the first Christmas that they didn't have all of us together under the same roof with them. I don't think that they were prepared to spend the holidays without all of us quite so soon. I know they made the best of it, but that Christmas was the beginning of yet another new existence for all of us.

After the holiday season, we were back in Florida with more changes taking place. I was waiting to find out if I qualified to receive financial aid for the medical assistant program at the vocational school, and Floyd went through a slow spell with his business but quickly recovered and was working crazy hours again. Sometimes, I felt guilty for still being in school while Floyd knocked himself out to find new customers. Sometimes, I wanted everything to speed up, so I could get a good job and contribute to our household income. However, other times, I liked being a teenager in school. Regardless, I couldn't get the right paying job until I finished school. It seemed as though there was a constant tug-of-war between my old life and my new one.

To break things up a bit and become more social with the other kids, I thought it might be fun to get involved in a few extracurricular activities in school. This idea, however, was met with no support from anyone. Doing other things at school meant spending less time with Jeremy. My mother didn't seem to be too thrilled about it. She never broached the subject, but her silence was clear enough to me. Floyd, on the other hand, made no attempt to hide his feelings about it. He came right out and said, "Look, either you be a mom and school's going to be second, or I'm going to take Jeremy, and we're going to move back to Maine."

Those razor sharp words were hard to hear from Floyd. I knew that I had made my decision in choosing to have Jeremy and to get married as a teen, but did it mean that I was to lose myself completely in the process? Did it mean that I had to give up everything that made me who I am to fit within all of the new roles that were expected of me?

Maybe it did. And even if it didn't, trying to juggle everything and, at the same time, feel like I knew who I was looking at in the mirror was tough. After all, I was still just a kid. I hadn't learned everything I needed to know to find the right balance in my life based upon those circumstances and everything I had experienced up until that time.

I did the best I could, but because of Floyd's ultimatum, I kept mostly to myself the rest of my senior year. I didn't want to become very close to anyone, because I didn't want to be accused of being a bad mom or do anything that would cause Floyd to take Jeremy away from me. I understood his reasons, especially because Floyd hadn't experienced much of the world either. He was only nineteen when we got married, and he hadn't learned enough about life to know that it was okay for men to be plugged into their families and have active roles in the rearing of their children. I could definitely see things from his viewpoint, but that didn't change the resentment I felt for having the fear of losing Jeremy looming over me.

On top of that, business had improved, and Floyd was back to working ridiculous hours. It didn't matter that he spent hardly any time with Jeremy or me, because work justified his absence. All he knew was the traditional image of the man going to work and being the provider for his family. It seemed to me that I wasn't entitled to the same consideration, and my only job was to be a wife and a mom; nothing more and nothing less. I wished that Floyd had understood that my love for Jeremy and him would never waver and had nothing to do with my need to figure out my own identity. I couldn't have loved them any more than I did, but how could I be the best mom that I could be and effectively teach Jeremy how to find his path in life if I didn't have any clue about my own?

I don't know how many times I thought to myself, *It is what it is*, telling myself I just had to do the best I could with the circumstances I had. So I kept forging on, trying to be a good wife and mom at home, as well as a good student in school. I'm proud to say that I graduated from high school that year with honors.

By that time, Mom was working regularly. This meant that she wasn't going to be available to watch Jeremy during my classes at vocational school. Although this presented a challenge, I really couldn't complain. Mom did us a huge favor by caring for Jeremy while I finished high school and giving us a roof over our heads. The truth was that she had already raised a family and had really stepped up to help me with mine. It was time for me to figure out how to find my own childcare.

I started my search, and through careful screening, I eventually found a good and qualified woman who was an ideal candidate for watching Jeremy while I was attending classes. She was a mother of two, and this gave Jeremy an opportunity to socialize and bond with other kids. Knowing that my son was in good hands, I could focus on getting through vocational school.

This letter is from my mom on my birthday:

Dear Julie,

Today you are nineteen years old. When I woke up this morning, I thought of you as you were nineteen years ago on that first morning after you were born. You were a beautiful, pink, fat-cheeked, bright-eyed little girl with one of the loudest pair of lungs in the nursery. So different from your long, skinny, dark-haired, quiet brother when he was born. You were just what I wanted, and I was on top of the world that day. There have been many beautiful and memorable days since then. Many days when your dad and I have felt the joy and pain of being parents. I'd like to recall just a few of those times with you today.

We lived in Amherst when you were born, and it was a terribly cold winter in a drafty, old parsonage, and I was alone so much with two small babies and often no transportation. I remember your first winter cold that developed into severe bronchitis. You had a high fever and could hardly breathe, and I thought for sure I was going to lose you. But the doctor came to the house and gave me medicine for you, and within a few days, you were back to your happy, healthy self. The thing I remember with delight while we lived in Amherst was your little treks over to Mrs. Crutch's house early in the morning after you'd gotten yourself out of the house and out of your diaper with an amazing silence and speed to end up having breakfast with the babysitter while I frantically looked for you. You knew exactly what you were doing and where you were going, and you still do today.

The year we lived with Gramma and Grampa Andersen was a very special year for us. Dad was away at Ann Arbor, Michigan, and would often write you and Mark little letters with stick figure drawings to delight and entertain you both.

You fell off the slide at the park and suffered a concussion and again gave us quite a scare, but it wasn't long before you were back making us laugh again. I often wondered if I had a little girl that year ... you were so determined to be "one of the boys" with Mark and Rick and would wear boxer shorts, T-shirts, and a baseball cap for days on end. The only time that I could get you in a dress was for church on Sunday and then only if I promised you could change as soon as you got home. You gave us another scare when you pulled the old dresser over on yourself by trying to climb up the drawers to reach something on top.

When we moved to Portland, you loved nursery school, and Mark envied you, all that great equipment and fun. You were growing into a very competent little lady who was a joy to watch as you gracefully danced in the Cameron School of Ballet one minute and diligently looked after your baby sister the next. You suffered over friendships, had a shoplifting experience none of us will ever forget (you turned yourself in). You had a very rough spring and summer the year you had mono, which was only made pleasant by our trip in the Winnebago that year. Breakfasts with Gramma and Grampa Valente and later our trips to Florida were some of the best times of those years in Portland. You grew to a lovely, sensitive, intelligent young woman, who single-handedly planned a beautiful wedding, gave birth to a healthy baby without the benefit of your family nearby, and then went on to finish high school and graduate with honors. You are amazing, but then I shouldn't be surprised. You have always done what you set out to do, and you continue to do that.

Here you are today, in Sarasota, Florida, married to a fine young man, the mother of a delightful two-year-old, and handling a tough medical assistant program at vocational school with poise and confidence. I am proud of you, your dad is proud of you, and your grandparents are proud of you. You have your whole life ahead of you and a lot going for you. We wish you the best of everything life has to offer, and we know you will make the best of it.

Sunrise, sunset, sunrise, sunset,
Swiftly flow the days.
Seedlings turn overnight to sunflowers
Blossoming even as we gaze.

Sunrise, sunset, sunrise, sunset
Swiftly fly the years.
One season following another
Laden with happiness and tears.

Love,
Mom and Dad

Waning Endurance

Vocational school was nothing like high school. The Medical Assistant Program was more structured, and it was steeped in clinical and administrative academics, which required unyielding commitment, comprehensive understanding, and meticulous attention to detail. I couldn't coast through this program out of boredom or because the work was too easy. I had to give it a 1,000 percent effort from beginning to end, to make sure that I learned everything necessary to be successful in that field.

I worked tirelessly the entire time and saw the results of my hard work when I graduated with honors, receiving a National Outstanding Student Award. I was so proud of myself for this achievement. The remarkable thing was that Mom and I were going after parallel interests, as we were both working toward the same professional goals and ended up taking our certification exam at the same time to become medical assistants. Although she had a strong background in nursing, Mom was looking for something in the medical field that would be fulfilling and allow her to use her expertise, but not in a position that was as demanding as an RN. This provided her the perfect balance between work and home.

Upon graduation, I found a job within a relatively short period of time that had a good starting pay, benefits, and Fridays off every week. This took some of the pressure off of Floyd, and I felt as though I was contributing to our life. Of course, many say that the job of being a wife and mom are the most valuable. I couldn't agree more. But being able to pitch in financially had a value all of its own and helped to make our life better.

Because Floyd's construction business had been holding steady with his regular commercial accounts and with the addition of my income, we were finally doing okay financially. We could afford our own day care, as well as an apartment of our own. It felt good to be able to stand on our own feet completely without needing his folks or mine to feed us, house us, or take care of Jeremy.

Then, just when we started to let our guard down, Floyd's business hit a really slow period and my income couldn't cover all of our expenses. I couldn't believe it. It was one step forward and two steps back. We were struggling all over again and getting financial help from my parents, who had their own expenses to pay. This was one of the reasons that Mom and Dad had been so fearful when I'd gotten pregnant and married Floyd so young. They didn't want us to be in these types of unstable predicaments, and they also knew that they wouldn't always be able to help us when we needed it. I hated that our life had often put pressure upon theirs.

I had hoped and prayed that Floyd's business would pick up, but it didn't. Things only got worse. Then we found out that Floyd's dad wasn't doing well and needed another surgery. The only way Floyd could get there in time to see him was to fly, which was yet another expense we couldn't afford. It felt as though the walls were caving in on us from every direction, but Floyd needed to get home to be with his dad quickly, and that had to be our number one priority.

Although Floyd made it there before the surgery, sadly, there were complications during the operation, and his dad didn't make it. This was extremely painful for Floyd. With all of our problems, it didn't seem like there was going to be any light at the end of this tunnel.

We were three months behind in rent, and the landlord sent us an eviction notice. It didn't matter that we were young and needed a break. The landlord had been patient enough and just wanted his money. I asked my parents and my grandparents for help, but they all said no. We had to figure it out for ourselves, so we started by making a payment arrangement with the landlord for the back rent. We hung in there and just kept fighting to survive

I worked hard at my job, but Floyd's business continued to fluctuate. Sometimes he had work for a couple of weeks, and then he wouldn't have any at all. The bigger and more established construction outfits were able to retain more customers year-round, but Floyd's business was still young and didn't have the client base the other companies had.

Living in the apartment was expensive, and I felt like each month's rent was going down the drain. It seemed like a big waste of money, and I wished that we could do things differently. I thought it would be wiser to just go out and find a cheap, run-down house for pennies on the dollar. Floyd could do what he did best and turn a place like that into something beautiful, and then our monthly mortgage payments would help to build equity in the house, giving us something to work with in our investment. This made more sense than pouring money into something we didn't own at all. But I didn't know how feasible my idea was, considering all of our problems.

Floyd and I talked things over and agreed that our future wasn't getting any brighter living in Florida. It was what we had needed for a while to help us out of our previous jam, and we were beyond grateful for that, but the writing was on the wall. Living in Florida long term wasn't the best option for us. We had to make a change.

Maine had always been our home, and we missed being there. Floyd knew more people in the Portland area and was sure that he could be more successful in business there than he was in Florida. We decided to move back, but we planned to do it in steps. Rather than packing us up and leaving immediately, Floyd thought it would make more financial sense if he went up first and stayed with his mother, while I moved back in with my parents until after the first of the year. That way, we could save enough money to get an apartment of our own and pay for the travel expenses for me to get back home with Jeremy. Being apart wasn't what we wanted, but it was the only thing that we could do until Floyd could find work and get established in Maine.

It seemed like everything was going to go according to our plan, especially when Floyd was offered work by a contractor there. But as usual, something got in the way. The contractor told Floyd he had solid work lined up, but when it came time for Floyd to start, the contractor didn't have anything for Floyd to do, and nothing ever materialized.

He was frustrated, I was constantly worried, and we missed each other. It was just too much, and we had to do something. Living apart from each other was not working for either of us. I refused to wait any longer—I managed to gather just enough money to fly home to Maine with Jeremy.

It was so good to see Floyd, but our problems hadn't gone away. His work was unpredictable at best, and saving money wasn't even an option.

I had no regrets. I knew that life wouldn't be a bowl full of cherries at the beginning, but I honestly thought that, as we grew older, we would find our way. I never imagined in a million years that we would find ourselves right back where we started, living check to check, barely making ends meet, and unsure of our future.

I couldn't let this dilemma defeat us. We had come so far, and we had worked too hard to let our situation get worse. Floyd didn't like the idea of me having to work, but we had bigger fish to fry. I immediately started looking and found a job at just the right moment, as someone happened to be leaving the office when I applied.

We didn't have enough for childcare initially, and since Floyd wasn't working, I suggested that he stay at home and watch Jeremy for the time being. I knew that this role reversal was hard for Floyd to swallow with his more conventional way of thinking, but we had to do what we had to do.

Eventually, I put away enough money to get Jeremy enrolled in day care, which left Floyd free to find his own work. The money was okay, and I could pay all of our bills, but there wasn't much left over for extras. Once Floyd was able to find a job, he worked some, but the construction business had a tendency to be seasonal, and the work was not consistent. It seemed like we had one mountain to climb right after the other during those days. We had been living with Floyd's mom, because his income wasn't steady enough and my pay alone couldn't keep us afloat. It was discouraging to finally be adults and still have to depend upon someone else's generosity. I felt like a failure, but I refused to give up and was determined that we would get ourselves out of this mess.

Later that year, Floyd got a job much farther north in Maine, in a small town called Machias. Machias had a population of less than 2,500 people. It took almost four hours to drive up there. I hated that he had to be so far away. But it was work, and we couldn't afford to be choosy.

The only time we could see each other was on occasional weekend visits. Sometimes, Floyd came home. Other times I went up to Machias with Jeremy. It was nice to have a mini-getaway. It gave us an opportunity to do things together that we didn't usually do, like eating out, going for walks, or sailing. The time away from each other also helped us appreciate one another and sparked a little romance between us during our visits, allowing us to reconnect. Every day wasn't ideal, but we made the best of it.

Although we intended to have another child to give Jeremy a baby brother or baby sister, we planned to wait until we were in a better and more stable position. The universe, however, had something else to say about it. During one particular weekend rendezvous, our second child was conceived.

The timing of this pregnancy was not great at all, as we were still living with Floyd's mother, and we weren't financially prepared to bring another life into our world. However, that didn't change the fact that I was over the moon when I found out that we had another baby on the way. I knew that Floyd was happy too, but he was feeling the pressure of our new circumstances, and it put a slight strain on our relationship.

By that fall, Jeremy was four years old and already attending nursery school. My little boy was growing like a weed and getting smarter every day. With the baby due in June, Floyd was trying to find other living options for us. We couldn't live with his mom forever, especially with two children.

Luckily, he had all of the necessary financial documentation from his business to prove that he was earning enough of an income to be eligible for a construction loan. This was just what we needed to start building a house of our own for our family. We would have a chance for something much better and more stable, rather than throwing our money away on rent payments that we could never get back. Of course, building wasn't going to be a quick process. We still had to get the loan first, and with things so uncertain, nothing was guaranteed.

In the meantime, Floyd continued to look for work during most of that winter, while working on the house without any income.

Nevertheless, we somehow made it through those months. I glided through my pregnancy and worked right up until the due date.

I had contractions and went into the hospital, but it was premature. The contractions stopped, and the hospital sent me home. The next day, my water broke after dinner, and I went into labor. Our beautiful daughter, Jessica, was born less than an hour after I got to the hospital.

We were supposed to go to Jeremy's nursery school graduation ceremony that night, but Jessica had already let us know that she was going to do things in her own time.

I took the summer off for my maternity leave to get my bearings and establish a new routine with my two children. Jeremy had spent a lot of time with a sitter or in day care when he was a baby, and I wanted to do things differently with Jessica.

I treasured every moment that I spent with the kids over the next few months, playing with them, watching them interact with one another, and noticing the delightful distinctions between them. By the end of summer, Floyd had already gone away again to a job site in Vermont and was only coming home on weekends. These remote projects were starting to weigh on my nerves, as I was tired of only seeing my husband on the weekends. The kids needed to see their dad too. He was missing all of the precious moments during their most formative years. Floyd wasn't even there to see Jeremy when he started kindergarten. This was a defining period for our son, and I had to experience it alone without Floyd. I wondered if our marriage would always be this way or whether a day would come that we didn't have to be apart from each other because of work and money issues.

Jeremy started attending school for half days in the mornings, and then he started daycare at a different location from his sister in the afternoons. Instead of taking a regular lunch hour from work to eat, I went straight over to Jessica's daycare center to nurse her daily. I was worn out most of the time, but I did everything that I could to make our life work, even if I had to be both mom and dad to the kids while Floyd was away.

I didn't have as strong a support system as I would have liked. I suppose some might have believed that I didn't ask for help enough, and there were times I thought that too. Floyd's mom put a roof over our head, my parents had done the same for a while, and both of our families had bailed us out financially more times than I could count. I asked, and yet, after a while, many of our relatives started saying no to us. Either they didn't have any more to give, or they had lost patience with us and wanted us to be responsible enough to solve our own problems. Deep down, I understood their reasons, but it didn't help my situation. Floyd's mother was phenomenal, but even she had to be getting tired of our constant setbacks.

Some days, I couldn't even see straight trying to balance it all, but I gradually found a workable rhythm within our schedule. I dared to think that I could finally breathe again.

Then Jeremy got sick. He was diagnosed with roseola. I didn't understand how this was even possible, and I didn't know what to do. Floyd was still at the same remote work site, and he was not accessible, so I had to handle everything on my own. I missed a couple of days from work caring for Jeremy, but I couldn't afford to miss more than that.

When I returned, I approached one of the doctors in the office where I worked, who happened to be an infectious disease specialist. When I told the doctor about Jeremy's unique symptoms, he said that what I had described (swollen tongue, peeling skin, and rash) was not roseola at all. He thought it was something more serious called, Kawasaki syndrome. When he showed me the details of this disease in one of his books, I was horrified and became really afraid for Jeremy. I felt alone.

My parents were in Florida, Floyd was somewhere in Vermont and out of reach, and I couldn't put all of this on Floyd's mother. She was still adjusting to life without her husband, and she had already done so much for us. I had to get a grip and pull myself together for my son, because he needed me.

The doctor wasted no time putting me in touch with a top-notch pediatric specialist in Portland. This disease was known to cause cardiac problems in some children. Kawasaki syndrome causes inflammation to the walls of the coronary arteries that control the blood supply to the heart, which can result in weakened arteries, blood clotting, aneurysms, and heart attacks. Apparently, there wasn't a lot of information on what causes it and only speculation that previous viruses in the system like strep could lead to it. It is a very serious disease, but it is also treatable. Knowing that, I could maintain faith that my boy would beat this.

My working in a doctor's office probably saved Jeremy's life. My employer was willing to do blood work and run an EKG, along with a few other necessary tests, at the office and at the hospital. I never imagined that my employers would do all of this without charging me, but they did. I don't know if I would have been able to swing it without their help.

The doctor put Jeremy on aspirin therapy, but he was just a little guy, and it upset his stomach a lot. I never knew from one day to the next if I was going to get a call from the daycare center notifying me that Jeremy was sick again from his treatment or having another negative reaction. The staff at the office where I worked was so supportive, but every time I had to leave work to go get Jeremy, I was a nervous wreck and wondered if I would still have a job when I got back.

I felt overwhelmed much of the time, trying to keep my job and do well while I was at work, nursing my daughter, caring for my son, taking care of the bills, and trying to keep a clean house—all while my husband was far away working at one job site or another. There were times that I wanted to scream because I was mentally and physically exhausted, and it would have been nice to have someone take care of me for a change. But that wasn't going to happen.

My kids needed me to be on top of my game, but how could I be the best for them when I was too drained to take very good care of myself? I had a husband, but he didn't even know what was happening. I felt like he was either too busy or too far away to check in between visits home to see how we were doing. It wasn't fair, and I was irritated with him for it. Maybe it was wrong to feel that way, but I needed a break from all of my roles, so I could sleep and recharge my batteries.

I thought that, if I could have a couple of days to breathe, think, and relax, then maybe I could return home rejuvenated with a renewed sense of myself, feeling healthier inside and out so I could be my best for the kids. I wanted to talk to Floyd about it, but as usual, he was out of state and out of touch, leaving me no way to discuss anything with him.

Perhaps I should have waited, but I was fatigued and overwhelmed, and it was just a matter of time before I would end up getting sick if I didn't figure something out soon. My only option was to ask my mother-in-law to watch Jeremy and Jessica for me so I could get away. Floyd was due home for that weekend, and she just needed to watch them for a little while until he got home. I worried that she would say no, especially if Floyd wasn't able to make it home. But to my surprise, she agreed.

When I thought about where I wanted to go, I remembered how much I had loved being in Machias when Floyd worked there. I decided it would be the perfect place for my two-day retreat.

Evidently, after I had left that Friday, Floyd called home to let me know that he was definitely coming home but was running late. Only his mother answered and told him that I wasn't home. Floyd was not pleased to find out that I had gone away for the weekend. When I got home, I half expected my mother-in-law to be upset with me too, but she didn't give me a hard time. She didn't come right out and say anything. But the expression that she had on her face, when she told me, "Here are your children," made me feel as though she respected me for taking care of myself for a change.

Floyd was not used to taking care of the kids for more than a few hours, and he didn't have the easiest time while I was away trying to stay on top of Jeremy's antibiotics and aspirin treatments, giving Jessica her bottle, and keeping everything else balanced. For once, he saw what I had to do when he was away all of the time. It wasn't a punishment, and I wasn't even thinking about it like that. I just needed to get some rest.

Floyd seemed frazzled when I got back that Sunday and he immediately said to me, "Please don't ever do that again!"

I understood how he felt, which was why I needed to get away from everything. I don't think he saw it that way, though. Clearly, we needed to talk, and that is what we did. Floyd didn't realize how much was on my shoulders when he was away or how worn out I was from it all.

We came to the decision that we would move forward with our idea to build our own house. Floyd also agreed that these trips to Vermont for weeks at a time were not good for us or our family, and he needed to stay closer to home.

The loan was approved. It took about six months before the house was done, but it was well worth the wait. Floyd made it beautiful, the way he did everything that he built. Living in a house that belonged to us made a huge difference. We were surrounded by the walls that Floyd had built with his own hands. We still had bills and a loan to pay off, but for the first time in a long time, I felt like anything was possible.

After some pondering, I thought that it made more sense for me to stay at home with the kids. Floyd was on board with that idea. We agreed, however, that I had to contribute financially too. We couldn't afford to live on one income. Then I came up with an idea that would address both issues. I could stay home and take care of Jeremy and Jessica, while providing day care services for other kids. This was a great way to contribute to our household income while spending quality time with my own children.

The following year, Floyd decided to take a job working for a window company, as we couldn't count on the construction business to sustain us. With two children, we needed a steady paycheck with benefits and health insurance. Floyd wasn't really happy doing that type of work, but he hung in there, while doing several side jobs at night. I definitely respected his work ethic and commitment to being a good provider. At the same time, though, I felt like time was slipping away, and Floyd was missing vital moments with his children and with me. There were times that I didn't think we would ever find the right balance between work and home.

Eventually, Floyd saved enough money from his window job to branch out on his own and start his own construction business again. I don't think he was ever meant to be caged by another company as an employee. He had so much to offer with his talent that doing his own thing was the most logical direction for him. Plus, it gave him the most passion. I supported that aspect of him, and I always believed in him, even when things were tough between us.

It took a while, but after several years, we were finally in a position to live like real adults in our own home without having to depend upon his or my parents.

We weren't alone very long. It seemed that once we had our own house, our relatives found themselves on our doorstep. It had become

Grand Central Station at our place, but oddly, we didn't mind it so much. We appreciated the help that had been extended to us during our times of hardship, and we wanted to pay it forward to those who needed us.

In 1990, Floyd decided that it was time to build an addition to the house to better accommodate everyone. But by the time the addition was completed, everyone had moved on. It was almost strange to have the house to ourselves and a bit awkward between us. At the beginning of our marriage, we didn't have time to focus on each other; we were an instant family and had to figure out how to function in our new grown-up world. After that, we were inundated with so many troubles that we didn't have the opportunity to really connect with one another. Then, once we finally got on track with our lives, we were so comfortable with people being around us all of the time that we forgot how to communicate with each other, and we didn't know how to interact in a one-on-one setting. It was bumpy at first, but through time and effort, we slowly found our way and started to reconnect.

I think the biggest challenge between us by that time was the way our roles were defined, with Floyd viewing our family through a traditional lens, while I had a desire for a more modern existence. I had dreams, but I'd never had the chance to pursue them, because we had immediate needs. I was grateful for the education I'd received and the resulting jobs, but the medical field was never my dream. Saying that I was pushed into it might be strong, but I was definitely nudged into being a medical assistant. It was a steady job that would generate a regular income with benefits. Considering that I was a teenage mother and a wife, there was a sense of urgency. I had to find a profession that made sense for our needs at the time.

Floyd, on the other hand, had had more opportunities to do what he loved, because his image of a good husband and father was a man whose primary focus was his profession. He always viewed domestic duties and child rearing as my sole responsibility. In other words, he would bring home the bacon, and it was my job to fry it up in the pan. The emotional nurturing that our children needed was also entirely on me. Floyd never fought me about working because we needed the money, but he always preferred me to be an at-home mom. I often wished that Floyd would have been more like my father, who took a more active role in raising us, despite having to be away at times for school and work. When Dad was home, he was plugged into our family by choice, not by obligation. There had been times when I'd felt like Floyd wasn't fully there with us even when he was home, which was hard to ignore.

Then my feelings of insecurity grew when a woman who was attracted to Floyd came into the picture. We had been married for about ten years, had our two children, and I was still in my twenties. Our marriage was not perfect, and after years of scratching and clawing to exist, take care of our children, and pay our bills, maybe Floyd was tired of it all. He'd stepped up to the plate when I got pregnant, and I'm sure that we were in love at the time, but this was the only life that we knew. It wasn't completely out of the realm of possibility that he might have wanted more for himself and felt saddled to us. Naturally, when this woman made her intentions known, I was scared that her carefree life would be more appealing to him than what we had together, and I wasn't sure that he would want to stay with us.

I decided that it was time to visit my parents in Florida for a while; I felt angry and desperate. Staying in Maine with those emotions consuming me would have been more harmful than good. I figured the best thing I could do was step away from the situation.

While visiting my parents, my mom wrote a letter to Floyd:

Dear Floyd,

I hope you will read this letter and accept it not as advice, but rather as an offering of love. Karl and I are your parents-in-law, but we think of you as a son and only want the best for you and our daughter.

Julie is here with us now, and we are pleased to have her, but we know that she is hurting. She has only told us briefly why she felt she needed to come to visit us at this time, but I know her well enough to know that she is going through a difficult time, a time that is both natural and to be expected for a young woman in her circumstances. She is, after all, only twenty-six years old and has been married ten years with two children. She also takes her responsibilities very seriously and loves her family very much. She is nonetheless an intelligent woman with a whole life ahead of her and wants to be able to express herself creatively through some kind of work. She doesn't know what that may be, but it is gnawing at her in much the same way you experienced before you wanted to start your own business. She needs recognition and appreciation for her talents.

She has a strong commitment to you and the children and does not want to jeopardize that, but she feels she can no longer ignore her own needs. One very important need for her is to be able to talk about her feelings. It helps her to deal with them and with what she wants to do.

We have always been a very communicative family. Julie needs to communicate her feelings and know that you are hearing her, not just her words, but the feelings. She needs feedback. Otherwise, it is as though she isn't taken seriously.

Successful marriages have low times as well as high times. Times when business is good and times when it is not good. But if you have built a good, solid base, you can weather those times.

I hope that, while Julie is here, she can rest and reflect on her needs. I know she loves you, and we love both of you. You have a marriage worth giving attention to, and if you do, it can only get better.

Love,

Mom

I had time to think with my parents completely behind me. While I was there, I realized that hiding from my problems wouldn't solve them, and giving up on my marriage was not going to be an option either. Floyd and I had gotten together under the most challenging of circumstances, and everything about our life was against all odds. I wasn't going to let an interloper destroy all that we had built over that decade, and I wasn't going to give up my husband without a fight—for our life, for our family, and for us. I would like to think that my mother's words meant something to Floyd, as well as my decision to trust that he would choose us.

Revising the Plan

As it turned out, 1990 proved to be another year of adjustment for all of us due to an array of unexpected circumstances. I had been working as a medical assistant in the medical department of an insurance company. This position was slightly different from the norm, because the company required me to have EMT training in conjunction with my previous experience. It was a good job, it was paying the bills, and it had benefits. After years of worrying and trying to make ends meet, it was a relief to get a paycheck that I could count on every week.

One morning, just as I started to pull up to the office where I worked, I noticed a huge commotion in front of the building. When I got closer, I couldn't believe my eyes. There had been a major accident, and it looked serious. I found out that a drunk driver had crashed his car. To make matters worse, he had his five young children inside of the vehicle with him. I felt heartbroken for the family, but also, I felt angry. This accident was so tragic and senseless. It should never have happened. Sadly, the driver, along with four of his five children died at the scene. The fifth child, who was only two years old, was rushed to the hospital, but the injuries were too severe. The baby was not expected to live.

The air in the office later that day was quiet and somber, and the ability to function was challenging for many. Especially the employees who had been outside attempting to assist the rescuers in caring for the children. Many felt the emotional heaviness of the entire ordeal. Death was never an easy thing to face with any person, but it was particularly difficult in this case, where innocent children were involved. I have to admit that it shook me up too and made me just want to hug my children. When I left that day to pick up Jessica from day care, I couldn't stop the tears from falling. I felt so grateful that my children were healthy and safe.

I had already picked up Jeremy and the three of us were on our way home. I felt so much better having my children with me after witnessing so much loss that morning.

We were almost to the house when I noticed one of Jeremy's friends out on his bike. Jeremy knew a boy from the neighborhood who shared the same first name. The two boys were inseparable and loved playing together. In fact, my Jeremy had just spent the night over at the other Jeremy's house. We didn't live that far apart, which made it easy for the boys to see each other whenever they wanted. Either they were at our place or his, but the other Jeremy's mother and I always knew where to find them. She and I were fairly strict about where we were willing to let the boys ride their bikes. They only needed to ride on one small portion of the road, and we didn't want them riding too far away from our houses. We both worried about the traffic in our area.

When I spotted the other Jeremy, I said to my son, "Hey, there's Jeremy. He must be on his way over to see you." I thought he was following us, but when we pulled in, he wasn't behind us. As soon as I parked, the kids jumped out of the car and went into the house.

Then, when I got out of the car, I heard a horrible noise and turned around to discover that the other Jeremy had been hit by a van. I looked up at the house and thought to myself that I was so thankful that the kids hadn't seen anything. It would have been too much for them.

I ran into the house and called 9-1-1 and then told my Jeremy to call his friend's mother. I made the kids stay inside, and I ran back outside to be with Jeremy, only to realize that his injuries were too severe for me to do anything. He had serious head trauma, and all I could do was wait with him until his mother arrived and pray that he would be okay.

There was so much commotion surrounding the area, that Jeremy's mother couldn't get through the traffic to see him. A part of me was actually glad that she couldn't get through, because a mother should never have to see her child on the ground injured like that.

Fortunately, the ambulance had already arrived and got Jeremy inside. Then, I found his mother and drove her to the hospital. This was such a horrifying day. I would never have predicted everything that had transpired earlier at work, but then to see this happen to the other Jeremy was unimaginable.

Jeremy survived, but he was in a coma for about five months. During that time, his mother had him moved to a reputable head trauma facility in New York, with the hope that he would have a better chance for recovery there. I took Jeremy to New York periodically to visit his friend whenever we could. The doctors suggested that talking to him would be helpful. They believed that coma patients could hear everything that was going on around them. Jeremy's mother was happy that we went and put us up during those visits to help keep our costs down. My Jeremy talked to him each time, hoping that his friend would open his eyes.

When he finally came out of his coma, the other Jeremy wasn't the same anymore, and it broke my son's heart. We tried to stay in touch, but his mother had to deal with knowing that her son was on his way over to see my son when the accident occurred, and I think it was too hard for her. Life was going to be completely different for that family, and she had her hands full with his health care.

My Jeremy wanted to be strong for his friend, and he handled everything extremely well. But I know that it was harder on him than what he revealed to the rest of us. I think that this was the first time my son had to deal with the reality of life on such a profound level. I wish I could have shielded him from the pain that he felt. But in that moment, a sometimes stark reality-that no matter how much we try to protect our children, we can't protect them from everything-was actually true.

Later that year, I decided to do some traveling, which had been difficult to do in earlier years. Money had always been so tight. We had taken a page out of my mother's book and figured out how to make it work on a shoestring budget. Now, we were finally in a better position financially to do many of the things that we couldn't do before, and every opportunity that we had to travel, we took. After all that had taken place in earlier months, I thought a trip would do everyone, especially Jeremy, some good. My sister, Karen, had just graduated from Bates College, so I thought that a road trip to Canada with her might be a great way for me and the kids to unwind and to celebrate her graduation.

We began our week in Toronto, where we were going to stay for a few days to see some Canadian sites. While we were there on the first day, we spent an afternoon visiting the Royal Ontario Museum, where we saw several fascinating exhibits. However, when we came out, we discovered that our car had been towed away. There was a mandatory law I didn't know about that prohibited parking on the street after 3:00 p.m. during the week. Who knew?

We had to go through quite a process to get our car back and pay the impound fee and the ticket. Once we retrieved it, I decided that our difficulty might have been a sign for us to move on, so we did right away.

We decided to go on to Cobourg, Ontario, to see some of our relatives who lived there, which was only an hour and a half away from Toronto. After a really nice visit, we drove almost three hours to visit Niagara Falls. It was a long ride, but well worth it. How breathtaking the falls were, especially at night. All in all, we had a great trip and it was just what we all needed.

The following year, when Grampa Valente's birthday came around, the whole family pitched in to have his name placed on the American Immigrant Wall of Honor at Ellis Island. I could see how our gift had really touched his heart. Tears rolled down his cheeks after he opened his framed certificate of honor, which included information about his Italian lineage. It was such a special moment for Grampa Valente and for all of us to share with him.

Later on, Floyd and I took our first real vacation together to Cancun, Mexico as part of a contractor group with most expenses paid for. It was the most relaxing trip ever. The flight was about three and a half hours, and there was only one runway that was rather short in length compared to other airports, but the landing wasn't too bad.

After we got off the plane and found our luggage in baggage claim, we boarded a shuttle that took us to the hotel zone where the majority of the hotels were located. The ocean was around us as far as your eyes could see. The sand was pristine white, the water was a captivating aquamarine blue, and the native residents treated the vacationers like royalty.

Getting transportation from here to there was easy with an endless sea of VW Bugs as the local taxi service to take you anywhere you wanted to go. The prices for everything were reasonable, and we had our choice of dance clubs that were open all night long, restaurants galore, and every cocktail you could imagine. This tropical paradise was everything I had dreamed of and more, giving us some time to enjoy each other on our first vacation ever without our kids.

Later that year, the kids and I joined my parents in Colorado for a wonderful family reunion with relatives from all over. It was incredible to see cousins and other family members that I hadn't seen for a while, and my kids loved being with everyone. It felt good to have the freedom to travel and to share new and exciting experiences with my children.

In the spring of 1995, my sister was overseas studying at the London Business School. My parents, Mark, and his wife decided to take a trip to England to visit Karen. It seemed like the perfect opportunity to join them.

Instead of booking multiple rooms in a hotel, we rented an apartment, which was the ideal setup for all of us. We had quality time together while enjoying some of London's attractions. We took a few day trips, and we ended up staying a little longer on the coast of Cornwall, having the best time ever.

In June of that year, we had a terrible loss in our family. Grampa Valente passed away. I knew he had been sick for a while, but he was feisty and full of life, and I'd thought he would get better. I guess I had never imagined a day when he wouldn't be with us. It was hard to say good-bye, but I was grateful for all of the time I'd had with him. He was the type of grandfather that all children should have, and I knew my world would not be the same without him. The family planned a special memorial service that was set to take place later in September as a tribute to an extraordinary man.

During the same year, Floyd and I purchased a small property on Center Pond in Lincoln, Maine. That is where Floyd built a camp for us. He transformed it into more of a second residence with all the comforts of home offering us an occasional escape from our normal schedule between work and our other trips.

Lincoln had a different and calmer way of life—a more relaxing atmosphere and a simpler lifestyle where everyone learned to slow down and appreciate family. I have to admit that this was one of our best decisions. Having this camp was like having our own little retreat or sanctuary where we could connect with ourselves and each other. We played card games or pool, went swimming, and read. It was so lovely there that we made plans to spend Christmas at the camp. With our many vacations and trips up to the camp, I couldn't believe how different life had become in so many positive ways. I still felt as though something was missing, but couldn't put my finger on what it was.

When the school year started in the fall of 1995, Jeremy was a sophomore, and we were looking into several different colleges. My son was the same age that I had been when he was conceived, and he was already planning his future. He was making a list of schools that were his top picks, as well as the ones that he thought he might like to visit. I loved helping Jeremy research the various features of each college, from the academics to the student life. I think that I was living vicariously through him during the process, while thinking of what I had missed when I was his age. I wondered what it would have been like to be a college student, and I was thrilled that he was going to find his path in life.

Then I started to realize that, just because I hadn't gone to college when I was younger didn't mean it was too late for me all together. Why couldn't I go back to school as an adult? My grades had been exceptional when I was in high school and while I attended the vocational school. Getting a degree might be what I needed to reach the part of myself that I had struggled to identify.

I looked into Andover College, as it wasn't too far away and had an excellent curriculum. But making the decision wasn't that easy. I went through a mental tug-of-war, trying to determine if it was even feasible for me go. I visited Andover College on two different occasions with the intention of enrolling but chickened out at the last minute both times. I worried that it would be too much money to spend on myself, especially having two kids that we needed to put through college. I hadn't completely given up on the idea, but I figured out that I was not ready yet, and I put my plans on the back burner for a while.

In the meantime, I started planning a trip to Italy to honor my grandfather, complete with language lessons at the local Italian Heritage Center. Floyd and I didn't want to be restricted to the typical structured vacation and itinerary that was filled with prescheduled activities. We wanted the ability to see the sites at our own leisure and travel to the various regions of Italy on our own timetable.

Italy exceeded my expectations with its charm and unique beauty. There was so much to see and so little time to see it all, but we did our best. We visited Rome, Pompeii, Sorrento, and my sister joined us in Florence. From there, we continued on to Pisa, Venice, and Cesuna, the village where my grandfather was born.

It was a small village resort of only six hundred residents, but during the busy times, the population could grow to almost six thousand. Fortunately, the tourist season had recently ended, so we weren't caught in the usual congestion, making the visit more fun for all of us.

My granduncle who lived there showed us the house where my grandfather was born, the shrine-like cemetery where my great-grandfather was buried, and several pictures of the family that we had never seen. Just like Grampa Valente, my uncle shared the most entertaining stories. Of course, some stories were easier to understand than others, but I loved his Italian accent. I could have listened to him speak all day long.

Our Italian relatives were so welcoming, and they were pleased to show us anything and everything about the area. Their English wasn't great. Nor was our Italian. But we learned a little bit from each other, and somehow, the slight language gap didn't matter. We found our own way of communicating, and it was a beautiful thing.

Our relatives took us to Asiago, a little town right next to Cesuna, which was popular for its delicious cheese. And then my granduncles showed us a large war memorial that represented where they'd fought during World War II. I thought of Grampa Valente so many times during that trip and wished he could have been there with us. On some level, I think he was.

Unfortunately, the day arrived that we were scheduled to leave our relatives, and I hated to go. They were such sweet and loving people. I knew that I would never forget them or how wonderful our experience was. There was no doubt in my mind that we would return to Italy to see them again one day.

After we got back to the states, I felt more than ever like I needed to make a change in my life professionally. After careful thought, I left the insurance company and returned to the doctor's office where I had worked before Jessica was born. I didn't mind that kind of work because it allowed me to help people, but somewhere along the way, I had lost my passion for the medical field.

The experience was not the same the second time around, and it seemed as though I was drowning in endless paperwork. This was a clear sign to me that I needed to get out of the medical world completely and find a job that nurtured my spirit.

I had always kept the books for Floyd's construction business over the years, but I hadn't had much real training or a business degree. Once again, my mind wandered back to the idea of going to college.

The one thing that I knew definitively was that I wanted nothing to do with the medical field anymore. It had been good for me when we needed the income, but the truth was that I'd never really and truly loved what I did. I think that I talked myself into loving the work for the sake of being successful at it.

The work I did for Floyd's construction company was only about supporting my husband; accounting wasn't on my list of life goals either. At least, if I got my business degree, I would have something to show for all of the hard work that I had done for Floyd over the years—validation that I was skilled enough in my contribution to his business.

I continued to go back and forth in my mind about attending college. Ultimately, I decided that I *could* do it. Floyd's construction business was holding its own, and we could afford it. I eventually enrolled at Andover College and started studying business. While I was working toward my degree, I volunteered at an organization called the Peabody House. At that time, it was a community service program that offered help to individuals living with AIDS. It meant a lot to me to do something valuable for others, and this turned out to be the ideal place for me to do my internship under the supervision of the volunteer coordinator. My time there was filled with a myriad of duties from learning how to work with various social service agencies to grant writing.

When the program was over, the Peabody House offered me a position. Though I enjoyed volunteering, I didn't want to stay on as an employee. I thought that it was best to decline their offer and continue with my classes.

I felt like I was meeting myself coming and going at times, with so much to do, and I needed a break. In May 1998, shortly before my graduation from college and Jeremy's graduation from high school, I went on a girls' trip to New York with Jessica, Karen, and my mother. The timing was perfect. Karen had come from England to attend Jeremy's graduation, and this gave us the opportunity for a weekend away together. Also, we were there in time to see the military ships coming in for Fleet Week. They offered several tours of the various ships, and we took a tour of an aircraft carrier as well as a submarine. During our stay, we saw a show in the city, but we couldn't leave New York without hitting a few shops. I really enjoyed having that time with just the girls, and I think they had a great time too.

Shortly after the trip, I graduated in 1998, receiving my associate degree in business, and Jeremy graduated from high school. I finished with the highest grade point average in the entire business program. There was no doubt that I was an overachiever. But it paid off. I finally had a college degree.

That same summer, to celebrate all of our achievements, Floyd and I planned a vacation with the kids to Arizona. My parents had a time share there and let us use it, which was much better than staying in a hotel. It was unusually hot, around 100 degrees, which was nothing like the temperatures in Maine. But without the humidity, it was definitely bearable.

The most incredible part of the trip was the Grand Canyon. We got there by train ride, and I was in absolute awe of its magnitude and beauty. All the photos I had ever seen did not do it justice. I took as many pictures as I could during our time there and at the places we visited on some of our day trips to capture all of the special memories we made.

As time passed, I became increasingly interested in faiths and belief systems that were different from what I had learned during my childhood. I was curious about the spiritual world and what impact it might have on my own life. So in January of 1999, I visited a psychic. It was an intriguing session, and I wondered if she had an authentic gift or if she was just trying to make a quick buck. I chose to be open-minded about it, and I listened to what she had to say. She told me a few things that may have applied to my life, but the one thing that stuck out in my mind was when she said that I was going to make a big decision. At first, I thought that she was referring to my having declined the Peabody House job offer, but that had happened already. So I wasn't sure if there was any merit to what she had suggested.

Around the same time, I was going to regular massage therapy appointments to help me with neck pain I had from a previous snowmobiling accident. My massage therapist made me feel really comfortable and always had something positive and encouraging to say, often telling me, "With your background, you really ought to do this." She suggested I check out the local massage school and consider the idea.

I didn't check into it right away. I waited for a while. Then one day when I was in the area, I stopped in and had a look around. I was surprised that the administrators were willing to interview me on the spot, but they did. And I signed up immediately to begin classes a few days later. It wasn't like me to make a sudden decision about something important like that, but my instincts were telling me to just do it. So I did. Then I realized that *this* was the big decision the psychic had mentioned. Hmmm.

I hadn't thought through all of the logistics when I signed up that day. I later realized that my school schedule, commuting between Scarborough and Portland was going to conflict with getting Jessica back and forth to high school every day. She wasn't driving yet, and Floyd's availability depended on the location and schedule of his work projects, which changed from day to day. It was going to be a challenge, but I was committed to doing whatever I had to do to make everything work. The funny thing was that I signed up without really knowing what was involved in the training. I did have some ideas, and I was eager to see where this new adventure was going to take me.

Later that same day, I got a disturbing call from my mother, who told me she had just been diagnosed with an ovarian tumor. I immediately started questioning her about it, asking what her doctor thought and what the treatment plan was going to be. She told me that her oncologist said that a tumor had certain characteristics that typically determined its type, and the characteristics of her tumor showed that it was most likely malignant. The doctor scheduled Mom to have surgery to remove it and planned to give her chemotherapy treatment after that. This was the last thing I had expected to hear about my mother, and it scared the hell out of me. I wasn't sure how to process this terrible news, but I wanted to be hopeful and strong for her.

Actually, my mother was the strong one. She had decided to be proactive and had no intentions of being defeated by some tumor invading her body. Mom started doing some natural things to support herself until she had to have her surgery. She tried some guided imagery work, practiced meditation, went to an acupuncturist, and added a plethora of herbs to her diet, while trying several other holistic approaches. These were all areas of healing that I would eventually learn, but Mom did her own research and tried everything that she could.

When the time came for my mother's surgery, they opened her up and discovered that the tumor was completely gone. The doctors were shocked. They had never encountered a case like my mother's—never had they seen a tumor of this type that wasn't malignant; nor had they seen one disappear the way hers had.

Needless to say, because the tumor was gone, she didn't need any chemotherapy, and I was so grateful that she was going to be okay. I don't know how receptive her doctors were to crediting her Eastern medicine approach as the reason she'd recovered, considering that Western medicine was all about conventional treatments and science. However, I'm sure that her case was still astounding to them.

After seeing what my mother had done to heal her body successfully, I gained some clarity within my own quest for enlightenment. I knew then more than ever that I was on the right path with my enrollment in massage therapy school. My mother had shed a whole new light upon what healing meant, and this was going to open up a new world for me.

During my off time from massage classes and between business projects, Floyd and I continued our visits up to Lincoln. We had made a few friends over the years and had fun swimming or snowmobiling with them, depending upon the time of year that we went up. At home, our lives were inundated with commitments and plans. When we went up north to the camp, we found a sense of peace within our surroundings and ourselves. We even seriously discussed the idea of eventually moving up to Lincoln to make the camp our permanent residence.

So, naturally, when Floyd announced that he intended to open a sports shop business up in the Lincoln area– I was surprised. I thought he was going to move the construction business up north with us, but apparently, that wasn't his plan. Floyd wasn't moving the construction business, and he wasn't going to let it go either; that income was our bread and butter. He was going to operate both businesses while they were in two different locations. How was that going to work?

We had finally found some balance in our lives, and I wasn't sure how spreading our lives thinner was going to affect the family or the happy way of life we had created. This whole thing was so out of left field, and it didn't really make sense to me. I was concerned that his new business was going to cause us more harm than good. But Floyd painted an attractive picture of his vision, and I could see that he really wanted it. What could I do? I was apprehensive, no doubt, but I prayed that Floyd's new endeavor wouldn't destroy the life we had worked so hard to build. I knew I had to support him by accepting his new dream.

When we sat down and talked about the ins and outs of the shop, we agreed that my part would be small and temporary. This was going to be Floyd's business, and I had my own career interests to pursue, from massage therapy to holistic healing. Plus, we didn't want this business to negatively impact our marriage. We knew that many married couples didn't survive working together on that level. I didn't have to be on the job sites with the construction business, but I would have to be at the shop to do what he needed. We had been doing really well as a couple, and we wanted it to stay that way.

The plan was for me to be there initially in a human resources capacity. I would ensure that Floyd had the right staff members in place who could perform their designated duties adequately, while adding value to the business. However, I wasn't interested in being actively involved in the front of the store, dealing with customers and merchandise. I just wanted to remain behind the scenes to address any minor office issues that the regular office manager couldn't handle until I wasn't needed anymore. If only things had worked out the way we had originally discussed.

We opened the sports shop in May 2000, and my role was anything but small or temporary. Almost from its inception, I felt as though Floyd had completely revised our well thought out plan. And the dynamic between us changed drastically with all of the hours we had to spend together dealing with shop issues. Our plans to move up to Lincoln were on hold. For one thing, Floyd still had his construction business, which we needed for our steady income until the shop started making a profit. And Jessica was still in school.

I just couldn't be excited about the business, because I was being drawn further and further into it, where I didn't want or plan to be. Floyd needed me to take care of the finances, the accounting, and the payroll. Although I took care of these areas of his construction business, I quickly learned that the retail business didn't operate in the same manner, which made the work more demanding. Reconciling accounts in the sports shop was entirely different from what I had known, and this was a problem for me.

Floyd was frustrated with me more often than not, and we found ourselves going head to head over one thing or another because I was having difficulty. My fears were playing out right before my eyes, as our business issues were not doing anything for our personal relationship. Floyd didn't have a clear impression of all that was involved in the work he expected me to do or how much time and energy I had devoted to it for all of those months when I wanted to be focusing on my own goals.

At one point, I made such a colossal mistake I didn't think I was going to get it resolved. I had no choice but to call a professional accountant to help me figure out what I had done wrong and fix the problem. The accountant was fantastic. She managed to get the books back on track and was more than willing to take over that role in the business, which lifted a huge weight off of my shoulders.

I wish that alone would have solved our problems, but it didn't. Floyd's primary focus was his business, and I was knee-deep in it, helping him with a number of labor-intensive tasks. He spent four to five days a week at the shop and would only come home on the weekends. We had spent enough time apart when we were young, trying to navigate through the first years of being married teenage parents with barely enough money for food. In many ways, it felt like we were right back to those nerve-racking days with Floyd choosing work over his family. Only this time, he didn't have to. We had a roof over our heads, money in the bank, food on the table, and each other. Floyd didn't have to be away from us, and he didn't have to spend every living, breathing moment in the shop.

Occasionally, I felt as though I couldn't breathe—like my emotional stress was coming out sideways on a physical level, which started with a severe case of tendonitis that developed in both of my arms. The pain was so excruciating that I couldn't work for six weeks until I was better. While stress could have played a small part in my tendonitis, I think that it was mostly from the volume of work I had been doing.

Then, to make matters worse, I discovered a lump in my breast shortly after that. I went for a mammogram only to find out that I had another lump that caused the radiologist much more concern than the one I had found. The doctor performed ultrasounds as well as an aspiration, and it was a matter of waiting to find out whether or not I had breast cancer, on top of the anemia and weakness that the doctor had also diagnosed.

I hated feeling vulnerable, but I was genuinely afraid of the outcome. I made bargains with God and made promises to myself that I would do better if it wasn't cancer, which was ridiculous. Why did I need the threat of cancer to motivate me to take better care of myself?

I started researching the effects of stress on the body, and I tried to take the attitude and approach that my mother had followed when she was diagnosed with her ovarian tumor.

Luckily, I was given a clean bill of health. But I knew then that these health issues had everything to do with the pressure I had been under. My body was telling me that I needed to slow down, though it took me a while to listen.

As if I didn't have enough on my plate, Karen planned to get married in April 2001. Although my sister and her fiancé, Dave, lived in England, they wanted to be married in Maine. This presented a few challenges, as they were trying to do most of their planning from England. To top it off, she changed jobs, and they had moved twice during the previous year.

In the end, she pulled it off and had a beautiful wedding, wearing our mother's gown. I'm glad that she was able to wear it, and I know my mother was proud to see Karen walk down the aisle in her dress.

Karen and Dave went on a Mediterranean cruise for their honeymoon, which should have been the time of their lives. A couple of days into the cruise, however, she ended up getting sick. The medication that the ship's doctor administered caused Karen to have a bad reaction, making her much worse. When she and Dave got back home, she remained sick for quite a long time. My mother was so worried that she went to England to stay with her for a few weeks and then her in-laws went after Mom returned to the states. They didn't think that Karen was getting much better, at least not enough to be alone while Dave was at work during the day, so she came to stay with us.

I tried to help Karen as much as I could, but the truth was that she didn't need me to mother her the way I had in the past, which created some tension between us. The mood was already intense in our house— between the shop issues and having to put our dog, Moose, to sleep the day that Karen arrived. It wasn't the greatest visit in the world, but it was cathartic for me to finally see that my baby sister wasn't my baby doll anymore and that she was a grown woman.

After Karen got better and returned to England, I started wondering if moving to the camp would have made our lives easier. It was what Floyd and I had discussed before he opened the sports shop. But we still had the construction business, and I had Jessica to consider. She had just turned sixteen and was only a little older than I was when my own father announced that we would be moving to Florida for his new job. Jessica had a nineteen-year-old boyfriend, and while we liked him a lot, I still had my concerns about the age difference. I never imagined that we would be living somewhat parallel lives, but it was strange how similar our circumstances were. Jessica had a job, she had her school friends, and she had her boyfriend. I didn't want to force her into making decisions that she wasn't ready to make because we needed to move and uproot her.

I knew how that felt, and I didn't want her to go through the same thing that I had. I was proud of Jessica because she wouldn't have fought us on the move had we pressed the issue. We had even discussed changing schools and in the end kept her where she was. I had a chance to do right by her, and that was what I needed to do.

Of course, staying only widened the gap between Floyd and me, with the proverbial elephant that was always in the shop with us. And the rest of the summer did not improve. Floyd wasn't budging, and I was starting to feel some resentment toward him for that. I didn't want to be mad at Floyd; I just wanted him to work just as hard for us as he did for that sports shop. Was that too much to ask? Was I being selfish?

I don't know, but what I did know was that our marriage wasn't going to make it if we kept up the way we were going. I felt that I needed to be at home to be available for Jessica and take her to the places that she needed to go. So my time at the sports shop was limited. My emotions were getting the best of me, and when Floyd came home on the weekends, he didn't understand why I couldn't be happy and why I was upset so much of the time. I remember Floyd looking at me like I was being irrational, when all I wanted was for him to wrap his arms around me and make everything all right again. But all he could think about was the sports shop.

Toward the end of that summer, again, I decided that I needed an escape from it all. I planned a very last-minute trip to England to visit Karen. My parents had already been traveling in Europe with Jeremy and this seemed like a great chance to catch up with them and to get out from underneath my turmoil. I guess I was really running away from my problems, as I had in the past. But I needed the break to think about everything and figure out what I could do to make our situation better.

Also, I thought that maybe Floyd would realize that he needed to make some changes too. I didn't blame Floyd for everything, because it had taken the two of us to build our life together and it had taken the two of us to reach our rough patch. We just needed to communicate better and find a way back to our plans, our dreams, and each other.

That wasn't going to happen if I didn't get a break. I prayed that the brief time apart would do us both good and that, when we were reunited, we would start fresh.

I also thought it would be a wonderful idea to include a visit to Paris in my itinerary. Jeremy and Jessica had been there already. Since I was quite a bargain shopper, I found a heck of a price on a five-day, all-inclusive package deal that took me to Paris and then on to meet family in England. It was the perfect mini-reunion. It felt great to see everyone, if only for a little while. And everything about the trip exceeded my expectations.

I had plenty of time to think while I was away. When I returned, I decided to give up my work at the shop and at the construction business. I had always been expected to assume a variety of roles along my journey—to be the good wife, daughter, mother, and employee. Every time I tried to define my own roles, something or someone always stopped me. Jeremy was grown, and Jessica wasn't too far behind. It was high time that I started carving out my own path.

I had put my dreams on hold more often than not to be supportive of my husband, to be a good mother, and to prove to my parents that I made the right choice to keep and raise Jeremy despite our adolescent circumstances. I needed Floyd to be the one to support my choice for once. I knew it wouldn't be easy for him, being more "old school" in thought and ideals, but he was going to have to figure it out for the sake of my sanity and the preservation of our marriage. If I could have gotten my massage therapy business started and generated a steady income, then my absence in the construction business wouldn't have mattered so much. Floyd didn't have to do it all, and we could have met somewhere in the middle.

I tried to branch out on my own, but Floyd continued to need my help, and I didn't want to leave him in a lurch. I wanted him to take over or hire someone to do what I had been doing for both businesses, and I was willing to stay long enough to make the transition smooth. But that didn't happen.

This went on for another six months; nothing had changed. I'd waited so long for the opportunity to have my own dream. I never regretted choosing parenthood, getting married, or supporting my husband. I did the kind of work that was necessary to ensure my family had the income and benefits we needed, but when was it going to be my turn?

I tried to balance everything to give Jessica the continuity at home that she needed and to be the supportive wife that Floyd needed. I kept up with my massage classes and hoped that the right opportunity would materialize. Then I found out that the assistant teacher at the massage school was not only from Lincoln, but she had also been practicing massage therapy there. What were the odds? This had to be serendipity.

Floyd and I eventually talked about our situation in depth, remembering the day we had first started brainstorming about how wonderful and peaceful our life would be living up in the camp together. It felt good to really communicate without the discussion being about the employees, payroll, or store merchandise. We listened to each other, and Floyd understood how much this meant for both of us.

We agreed that I needed to put my massage business plans on hold for a little while longer because we couldn't just drop everything with so many loose ends to tie up first. Floyd had to deal with his construction business and I needed to be home in Scarborough for Jessica until she graduated from high school. I wanted her to have the best senior year possible, enjoying every experience to the fullest without the pressure or worry of having to leave before she was ready. Then, when we knew that she was set for college, we would relocate to our camp.

Floyd was going to continue running the shop. I got a temporary office job. It was a good compromise that I could live with. I didn't mind postponing my plans yet again because I felt like we were back on the same page working toward the mutual goals we had originally envisioned. It seemed like our plan was going to stick this time. Floyd and I were going to get back on track, and I was going to have something fulfilling of my own.

Over the following months, I continued to feel hopeful for the first time in a long time. I imagined what it would be like to live at the camp permanently, spending time with the kids there, socializing with our friends, and reconnecting with Floyd.

At the same time, a part of me was sad; Jessica was growing up so quickly, and she was exploring her own future. This was another reason that it was essential for me to figure out what was next, so Floyd and I could smoothly acclimate to our new existence as parents of adult children and remember what it felt like to be a couple again.

Feeling optimistic, I approached Floyd about six months before Jessica was due to graduate. "So, how are things looking to move up north?" I asked.

I expected him to say that he had been making arrangements in his construction business to either sell it for a good price or hire someone to run it and that we were right on schedule. I had never anticipated what he actually said. He told me that he couldn't see us moving up there at all because of our financial situation. What financial situation?

Floyd admitted that the shop had been dreadfully slow, and business wasn't going as well as he had expected. He went on to say that he was sinking more and more money into it, building debt rather than profits. Floyd told me that if we kept the shop open, we would just continue to dump more money into it, and we would never recover. If, on the other hand, we closed the doors permanently, we could get loans or liquidate to help us pay off the existing debt. I was shocked to find out how bad things had become.

Although I had never been thrilled about the way the sports shop business had come crashing into our lives, I'd wanted it to work for Floyd's sake. It meant a great deal to him. Plus, the prospect of keeping the shop as Floyd's primary business, with my impending massage practice supplementing our income made our "castle in the sky" idea of living at our camp more realistic. I think that I was in denial about how poorly the shop was doing and how it had rendered so much debt. Floyd said that it was so bad that bankruptcy was a real possibility.

The look on his face as he reluctantly shared the news with me said it all. I think he had been waiting until the last possible minute to tell me what was going on, because he had hoped that things would turn around before he had to say anything. Now it had reached the point of no return. Obviously, we were going to do whatever was necessary to protect our finances, which meant we would have to liquidate as many assets as we could to pay off the debt.

It also meant that we wouldn't be able to move up to Lincoln. We couldn't afford to lose the kind of income Floyd's construction business generated. Even then, there was no guarantee we would make enough from that business to cover everything we needed. Moving the construction business when it was thriving wouldn't have been smart either, as we had no way of predicting how successful the business would be farther up north.

I could feel my dream slipping away yet again. This time, it was compounded by the guilt I felt. Floyd's dream had fallen apart, and I'd walked away from the shop, leaving Floyd to deal with it on his own. Hearing his news was too much for me to absorb. How could it have been wrong for me to want my own dream after sacrificing everything to make sure that Floyd could have his? Maybe the shop wouldn't have failed if I hadn't left, but I don't think our marriage would have survived if I had stayed.

As much as I wanted to take responsibility for my part, the economy in that geographical area had tanked, and it would have taken Floyd, me, and a small army to keep that store afloat. The only thing that was left for us to do was to keep the shop going for as long as we could to prepare for its inevitable closing, in hopes that we could raise enough funds to wipe away our debt.

In February 2002, we closed the sports shop, and we barely skated by the doors of bankruptcy, leaving us nothing in reserve and having to start all over again.

Floyd and I were extremely disconnected at that point, and I was feeling the weight of my daughter leaving the nest. Jessica was ready to sprout her wings to fly, and the thought of living without any children in our home left me questioning my identity again. I had built an entire life around being a mom. Who would I be without my children? I knew that motherhood didn't end and that I would always be Jeremy and Jessica's mom, but my role had shifted and they needed to build their own lives. What did that mean for my marriage?

I felt less confident about myself as an empty nester, but I didn't want to sit around and wallow in my insecurities. I needed to do something to gain some awareness about myself, my emotions, and my fears. So I started reading as many books as I could on spiritual growth. I attended a few insightful workshops and began yoga. Everything that I learned pointed to one thing—I needed to find my own inner strength and stop defining my worth by my roles as a mother and a wife. In other words, I needed to figure out who I was and get comfortable looking at myself in the mirror.

My mind was reeling with a mountain of thoughts. September 11 hadn't been that long ago, and I couldn't help but remember the tragic loss that occurred as a result of acts of terrorism that were beyond our control. I had been in New York City only three years earlier. What if we had been on top of the World Trade Center when all of that had transpired? The thought of it was almost more than I could bear.

We had been living in a world where people have the attitude, "Why do it today when we can put it off until tomorrow?" Let's face it; we have all done that.

Floyd and I spent years trying to figure out how to put food on the table, where we would live, and how we would pay our bills. Then, once we became solvent, with a steady flow of income from the construction business, we got complacent in our cushier way of life. We forgot what it meant to appreciate every moment we had together, and we put off important goals because we thought, as many people do, that we'd always have tomorrow.

When Floyd threw himself into the shop, he didn't think that he was canceling our plans to make the camp in Lincoln our home. He was just putting things on hold indefinitely, figuring that it would eventually happen one day. This was an easy rut to fall into. Many people think like that.

The problem was that I waited all of those years to pursue my goals because I felt I had to in order to build a life for my family. I would never be sorry for putting my family first, but Jeremy and Jessica weren't kids anymore, and there was no reason why I had to wait any longer.

I had been getting my training in massage therapy and energy healing for a while, and I was ready to put those skills to use. My friend, Edna, from the massage school was going to be traveling which meant her job in Lincoln was available. The position was at the hospital as a massage therapist in the rehab department.

This was the opportunity that I had been waiting for and with all of our other plans getting derailed, I didn't know if I would ever get a chance like that again. Taking the job was a no-brainer.

I remembered a list of long-term goals Floyd shared with me when we were dating. I'd played an integral part in all of those goals that he'd achieved—from getting married and having a family to building his own home and running his own business. Before I had a chance to pursue my goals, he'd added a new objective to the list with the sports shop. I think that everyone presumed I didn't have any of my own goals. So when I mustered up enough courage to start taking steps toward my interests, it was met with some skepticism and resistance.

I couldn't keep playing into that way of thinking because, every time someone doubted me, I doubted myself. Then it was no longer about whether or not Floyd supported my dreams; it was about whether or not I believed in myself enough to move forward. Coming to that realization made me see that I needed to follow through with my plan. Though I wanted him to believe in me and support me in my choice, I needed to make this move anyway.

After Jessica graduated and left for college, I took the massage therapist job at the hospital in Lincoln. I stayed up there on my own at our camp during the week and spent weekends at home with Floyd. I hoped that my family would respect me for finally biting the bullet and doing something for myself.

Most of all, I hoped that Jeremy and Jessica would learn from my experience by taking their time to grow up. I wanted them to discover their own identities in their own time before they had to put others first. I wanted them to know that they didn't have to sacrifice one area of life for the other and that they could be successful both personally and professionally. It had taken me years to learn that lesson.

Jeremy and Jessica have always been different from one another. Jeremy always seemed to know which direction he wanted to go, and it was an easy path to get there. Jessica was always more determined and headstrong. She needed more room to grow, and she needed more time to figure out precisely what she wanted.

The only thing I've ever wanted for them was to be true to their own spirits, whatever that meant. And I wanted them to be educated enough that they could make their own fully informed decisions about what they wanted for their lives. I knew what it meant to make decisions before I was old enough or mature enough to understand the consequences of those decisions. I was lucky, because despite the challenges of my consequences, I got the greatest gift of all with Jeremy and Jessica. Not everyone is so lucky.

Although Floyd had been a bit of a caveman when it came to me working outside of the home, accepting it only out of financial necessity, he had evolved and changed his stance by the time Jessica was ready to step out into the world. He knew that she was entering a different society under different circumstances from those that Floyd and I had known, and he knew that she would be okay. Maybe his growth with her helped with us.

Floyd and I had been through it in ways that made both of us question if we could sustain our marriage. The odds were definitely stacked against us considering how we started. The thing is that loving each other was never an issue. Maybe that is what held us together through so much upheaval, and maybe that love is what enabled Floyd to be okay with my choice to stay in Lincoln to cultivate my business while he remained in Scarborough.

With the kids living their lives, we were learning how to be a couple again. It wasn't going to be an overnight process. It took a few years for us to get the hang of it, but we were well on our way, and I was finally doing something for me.

Fragility of Body and Spirit

Jessica had gone off to Connecticut for college. Then she moved back home to live with Floyd for a while. Having someone in the house made him feel less lonely. I continued with my massage therapy job in Lincoln, staying at the camp during the week and coming home to spend weekends with Floyd.

I was starting to see a different version of Floyd emerging over the course of that year. We spoke on the phone frequently, and it reminded me of the old days when we were kids and I still lived at home with my parents. We'd had some of the best conversations when Floyd was working on the attic in my house. It was during that time when we had first become friends that a solid foundation had been established for the love that grew from that friendship. I started to feel that synergy growing between us again while I was in Lincoln, and it felt like we were getting back to the core of what had made us work in the beginning. From there, our relationship grew deeper. The time we had apart was probably good for us in the long run because the money that I had earned in Lincoln, combined with Floyd's company revenue, helped to put us back in the black. Plus, we spent a significant amount of time just talking and remembering without any pressure.

But after a year, we'd been apart for long enough. It was time for me to go home, start a new massage practice, and live full-time with my husband. We celebrated our twenty-fifth wedding anniversary in 2004 and broke ground for the new home that Floyd was building for us in

Gorham, Maine, which was completed in July of that year—another new beginning.

During that year, I had trained hard to run in a five-mile race in November, which I finished successfully. I was in better shape than I had been for years, feeling strong, fit, and toned.

A few days after the race, I was scheduled to have elective surgery for a hysterectomy. It was supposed to be a routine procedure—something that doctors had been doing for years. However, my operation took a left turn into a window of complications, and it was anything but routine. The surgeon made the first incision through my navel, and as he was moving through that narrow corridor along my stomach, he accidentally nicked my bowel, causing a series of severe problems.

I had to go to the ER twice in less than two weeks. After endless poking and prodding, I received a diagnosis of peritonitis. This was a bacterial infection within the membrane lining my inner abdominal wall that originated from a complication during my hysterectomy. It was too serious to treat with antibiotics, and I had to have emergency surgery, resulting in a prolonged recovery period.

Needless to say, I took time off from my massage therapy practice to heal. I imagine an experience like that would have been hard for anyone, but I felt helpless, humiliated, and angry that the surgeon's mistake had caused me so much harm.

I was in the hospital for eleven grueling days, losing weight, losing muscle tone, and losing sleep. The hospital was the worst place for me to be to get better. The doctors and nurses barreled in and out of my room multiple times throughout the day and night. I don't know how many times I had finally started to drift off to sleep only to be awakened by loud beeping or someone else wanting to take my temperature, check my vitals, or ask me what my current threshold of pain was on a scale of zero to ten. The food wasn't appetizing, and after the operation, my diet was extremely limited, with numerous food restrictions.

That wasn't even the worst part, as privacy was nonexistent in that place. The staff asked the most invasive questions about my biological functions, and I had to answer them so they could determine the level of my progress. I couldn't wait to get home and be in the privacy of my own home. This was extremely hard for me. But in time, I healed and got back on my feet.

A couple of years had passed, and it was hard to believe that I was the mother of two grown children. It was even more mind-boggling when they both found spouses with whom to share their lives. My firstborn married a lovely young woman from Massachusetts named Sarah in February 2006. Floyd and I couldn't have been more proud of Jeremy or happier for their union and the new life that they were about to begin. My boy had become a twenty-six-year-old man and was making his mark upon the world.

The year continued to be flooded with wedding plans, as Jessica had found the love of her life and would be walking down the aisle. In September 2006, my sweet Jessica became a wife. We were pleased with her choice for a husband, and Eric was a great addition to our family. We knew that our daughter would be okay as we finally let go of the little girl she once was.

I think that one of the most riveting parts of watching my kids navigate their lives as adults was when they started having babies of their own. When I looked into the mirror, I didn't exactly see the typical image of a grandmother. I was younger than many that I had known. It didn't matter though. I loved the addition of that role in my life, and my heart was overflowing with love for my grandchildren. My kids had their own individual ways of parenting—some techniques that originated from our household and some that came from them. I did my best to respect their boundaries and only offered advice when asked. It was important to me to let them have their own independence without feeling like I was hovering over them with unsolicited suggestions.

In December 2009, when Jessica's youngest son was eighteen months old, she took a fall down the stairs while holding him in her arms. With inherent motherly instincts, she did everything she could to shield him from the impact of the fall, which kept that rugged little boy from getting anything more than a couple of minor bumps and bruises confirmed by a CT scan.

However, Jessica wasn't as lucky. She ended up breaking her ankle in three places. The doctors kept her in the hospital that night and scheduled her for surgery the very next morning. When it was all over, they had put two metal plates and four screws into her ankle. The doctor fit her for a cast, and Jessica was going to have a long recovery time until her ankle healed completely.

Eric's mother, Judi, realized that, with Eric at work during the day, Jessica wasn't going to be able to do everything herself. Judi decided to move in with them temporarily to help Jessica with the kids and anything that she needed while she was out of commission. It would have been easy for me to swoop in to take over for my daughter, but the fact that Eric's mother was willing to step in spoke volumes of her affection for Jessica. I didn't want to interfere with that. I thought that Jessica needed this time to bond with her mother-in-law, and it would be best for me to give their relationship some room. I was grateful to know that Judi cared so much for my daughter.

Unfortunately, I think that Jessica might have misinterpreted my motives for stepping back, which caused some friction between us for a while. As a mom, it was hard to determine when it was okay to impose myself upon my kids and when it was prudent to leave them alone. If I had followed my heart, I would never have let my children out of my sight for the rest of forever, but that certainly wasn't practical or rational. They needed to live their own lives, and I truly wanted that for them. I simply had to be smart enough to know how to give them the space they needed or at least give it my best effort. This awareness was in line with my ongoing quest to establish my own identity without deeming it necessary to be a helicopter mom.

Those first few weeks, especially during the holidays, were difficult for Jessica—from the physical pain of her injury to not being mobile enough to do the things she was used to doing, like playing with the kids, getting ready for Christmas, working, and doing things around the house. However, in time, she got much better and was able to get back to her life.

Then a year and a half later, something devastating happened that shattered my daughter's heart and changed all of our lives. Jessica found out that her best friend, Karolina Kurka, had been working out in the gym when she'd had a sudden brain aneurysm. Jessica drove right away to Mass General in Boston, where Karolina had been taken to have surgery. The surgery lasted eight hours and when Jessica left the hospital, Karolina still hadn't woken up. She was a vibrant twenty-seven year-old who everyone loved, and she was planning to be married in a couple of months. Sadly her wedding day never arrived. Karolina Kurka died on July 21, 2011.

My daughter was impacted by more than the loss of her dear friend as she started taking inventory of her own health. She had been suffering from a series of headaches for about five years. Perhaps it was normal to feel that type of fear after the way that Karolina had died, but Jessica's fears seemed to stem from something more far-reaching than mere anxiety. It was as if she had a sixth sense about what was happening within her body, and she refused to let it go.

Jessica made an appointment with her primary doctor to request an MRI. If nothing else, she needed to know one way or the other to ease her mind about what she had been thinking and feeling. Instead of honoring her request, the doctor attributed Jessica's worries to her grief and treated Jessica like she was being silly—also stating that she couldn't justify sending in a claim to the insurance company for an unnecessary procedure. Jessica left that appointment feeling invalidated and even more adamant about the matter.

Eric would have done anything for Jessica, so a couple of weeks later, when he was scheduled for his own doctor's appointment, he took that opportunity to visit Jessica's doctor as well. Eric told the doctor that he didn't appreciate the way she had dismissed his wife's concerns, and he firmly insisted that they get another opinion as soon as possible. The doctor gave in and set up a referral for Jessica to see a neurologist in January for an evaluation.

After months of waiting for an appointment, Jessica had a full neurology evaluation on a Tuesday and an MRI on Wednesday that same week. Thursday she received a call from the neurologist to let her know that she had a brain tumor. Jessica immediately called me to let me know. My daughter knew something wasn't right. Whether it was intuition or Karolina giving one final gift to Jessica, she knew. And thankfully, neither she nor Eric gave up until they could get confirmation.

Knowing didn't change the fact that my baby was about to face the biggest crisis of her life, and there was nothing that I could do to fix it. I stood in my kitchen, barely able to breathe or even move my feet after that telephone call. I couldn't understand how something like this could happen to her, and I had to face the real possibility that I could lose my daughter.

What about her husband and her children? I wasn't prepared for this, and I couldn't accept that possibility, no matter what any doctor said. I had to believe that she would survive. I just had to believe that.

Floyd drove Jessica to the neurologist's office, where she met Eric to discuss the results of her MRI with the doctor. Together, they made a plan for what was going to happen next, and scheduled Jessica's surgery to be performed two weeks later.

The neurosurgeon indicated that, because her tumor was positioned in a sensitive location of her brain where her movement, speech, and vision could be impacted, she would have to be awake for the middle portion of the surgery. This was called intraoperative brain mapping. While Jessica was still sedated, they were going to wake her up to ask her questions, have her count, show her images, and monitor her responses to map out the functional areas of her brain. Then, they would put her back under, so they could remove the tumor, while avoiding contact with those functional regions to decrease the chance of any deficits.

Even if the surgery was successful, barring any major complications, there was still a slight chance that she could be subjected to some post-op loss of function, but there was no way to predict the outcome.

During those weeks leading up to her surgery, Jessica had to get an EEG. This test helped the neurosurgeon determine that her body could handle the surgery and indicated that she'd probably had the tumor for about five years—the amount of time she had been having her headaches. Also, Jessica started getting her affairs in order—from writing a will to making final arrangements in case of her death.

The only thing that Floyd and I could do was to respect her decisions and give her and her family as much emotional support as possible. I was crumbling inside, but I couldn't show Jessica how afraid I was because it wasn't her job to make me feel better. I had to be the mom that she needed without her worrying about me or anyone else.

Before we knew it, the morning of Jessica's surgery had arrived. I was doing my best to remain hopeful; we all were. But the mood in the pre-op room was awkwardly intense. Jessica was amazing, trying to show everyone how strong she was, but I knew that she was scared. She was surrounded by as many relatives as could fit into the room, and we tried to keep it light with jokes and laughter to let her know that we had faith that she would be okay.

Just before the staff rolled her away, I looked at Jessica and said, "See you on the other side." Those were the last words that my daughter heard me say.

I mulled over those words obsessively, wondering if I had said the right thing. What did she think that I meant? And would the universe interpret my words to mean that heaven was on the other side of surgery or would it mean recovery? It was absurd, but I irrationally thought that my chosen words had the power to control the results of her surgery. I guess that I had a lot of thoughts that didn't make logical sense while I sat in the waiting room listening to some of the doom and gloom that I heard. But I generally stopped myself to focus more on being positive, as hard as it was. I put my headphones on to tune out the rest of the room and listened to relaxing music to keep myself calm.

When the surgery was over and Jessica was taken into recovery, we still had to wait a while before we could see her. It seemed like an eternity. The doctor let Eric in to see Jessica in recovery first, but Judi and I snuck in through an open hallway just to get a peek at her. I needed to see her face.

She had a blank expression on her face, and we couldn't tell whether or not she knew who we were. The doctor said that Jessica's motor skills were fine, along with the movement of her hands, arms, and legs, but she did have some difficulty with her speech. It was going to take time for Jessica's brain to communicate to her speech receptors. Though she had some difficulty with memory, she was able to recognize Eric right away.

The doctors and nurses felt that Jessica had exceeded expectations in her recovery. The MRI showed that they removed the entire tumor, and they were just waiting on some test results to find out more information about the tumor itself.

Sometimes, Jessica was fuzzy and had unexpected memory issues. One minute she might not be able to recognize you, and then a half hour later, she knew exactly who you were. She continued to have issues with speech. She got some numbers backward or mixed up other things, but Eric worked with her, using different tools to help Jessica communicate better. And they scheduled her for speech therapy.

Jessica had always been good about drinking water before, but she wasn't drinking enough after the surgery. Eric had to find creative ways to get her to drink more which was important for her medication intake and her continued recovery.

The doctor seemed like he was dragging his feet a little bit and was going to make Eric wait a week until her follow up appointment to find out exactly what was going on with Jessica's pathology results. But Eric had a will of iron and wasn't going to wait a week. He wanted answers to get Jessica whatever treatment she needed as soon as possible.

After some pushing, Eric found out the pathology report indicated that her tumor was mostly a stage II cancer. There was a portion that was stage III as well. Chemotherapy was the best option to eradicate any residual cancer cells in her body.

Jessica's speech therapy began and was scheduled to last for approximately six weeks. Because I knew my daughter, I paid attention to every nuance of her personality to see what seemed different and how she was improving. Sometimes, she seemed a little flat and detached. Other times, I could see the sparkle in her eyes. I think her brain was still learning how to react to different stimulus and retraining itself in a way. It was going to take time, and there may have been some differences in Jessica after the surgery that wouldn't change. We would have to get used to those differences in her personality.

The other issue was that, because she'd had brain surgery, Jessica was a prime candidate for seizures. She had to take anti-seizure medication to prevent any abnormalities from occurring and triggering a seizure, as these could be more damaging to her brain.

The oncologist decided that Jessica would benefit most from oral chemotherapy for one year. She was going to have to take a pill for five days straight once a month. Although Jessica wasn't great at swallowing pills, and these were definitely horse pills, the upside was that her side effects would be minimal, and she wouldn't lose her hair. We were taking every victory, big or small, as it came with gratitude.

However, the pill form of her treatment was not as effective as the doctors had expected. Ultimately, she had to receive her chemotherapy through hospital infusions.

Eric's mom and I tried to coordinate our efforts, with her doing more in the house—laundry, dishes, and the like—while I was in charge of transporting the kids to and from preschool. My plate was full, between that and doing Jessica's work for Floyd's construction business while she was out. I will say that Floyd and I did much better working together this time; we didn't raise our voices at each other too much, which was progress.

There were times that I felt that I couldn't do enough to help Jessica. Then other times, I was exhausted from trying to keep on top of things. Eric had his hands full and I wanted him to have some down time to relax. At the same time, I knew I would have more to do when Eric returned to work, as Jessica couldn't be alone. I was wound tight; I didn't feel like I could let my guard down for a minute. I hoped that I was being a good source of support for my daughter, but I sure wanted my own mother to talk to while all of this was going on. Fortunately she was coming to Maine for a while to help me out, and that was just what I needed.

It was astounding to see Jessica's progress. In March, I was showing her pictures of people in a photo album to see who she remembered. By the middle of April, she was reading, writing, and remembering everyone—and her speech therapist was ready to discharge her. She was scheduled for an MRI to see how things were going, and the results looked good. Every month, Jessica improved more, and every day, I felt enormous gratitude that my daughter had lived and recovered. I couldn't help but think of Karolina, as everyone did, because Karolina had saved Jessica's life. She was the best friend that Jessica could ever have, even from beyond.

Transcending through Resilience

On more than one occasion, my mother has faced the mystery of her fears while combating her body's demons and healing her soul with and beyond the realm of science. Her steadfast courage has been an unexpected yet deep-seated source of wisdom and enlightenment—an awakening of growth that has given me more than I thought I would ever know.

With the grave injuries to his childhood friend, my son learned at a tender age that the design of life is not guaranteed and it could all change within a moment. He waved good-bye to an existence that was forever altered before any child should ever have to face this aspect of life. Jeremy carried the stamp of that sorrow into his future before he was ready to release that part of his past. But through the billows of time and through his desire to prevail, he was able to let go and move into his own bravery while walking into the horizon of his new love.

My daughter survived the most frightening and harrowing experience at the heels of the most profound loss. Jessica walked through the broken shards of physical and mental transformation during the most insurmountable phase of her journey. The most impactful experience for me was to see her revert to my little girl—needing her mother once again. I never knew where to draw the line, because the linear boundary between parent and child has always been hazy. How often adults feel like children, wanting their parents to pamper or nurse them back to health when illness strikes.

I've often wondered if this was how Jessica felt, only on a much larger scale. She faced mortality head-on and won her battle, but it wasn't without extreme cost. She lost her most treasured friend, yet it was that loss that saved her from the clutches of brain cancer.

If I could have protected my children from all of that pain, anguish, and trepidation, I certainly would have. But nothing I could have done would have changed the circumstances.

How hard was it for Jessica to find her confidence again after seizing every ounce of strength that she had to push through her recovery? Even at age twenty-seven, did the gravity of her condition strip away her adulthood, leaving her to start all over again?

I can't recall the number of times I have regressed in my life because I began my adult journey as a child. Whenever things went wrong the only consistent part of my being that I had to cling to was my childhood. My parents may have lost their patience with me more often than they care to admit, and perhaps they attributed my ongoing adolescence to my premature leap into an adult world that I wasn't ready to join. However, their love for me never diminished, even when they had to show me the tenacious love that I was not prepared to receive.

There have been moments when I have reluctantly shared that same decisiveness—with Jeremy to bolster his confidence and with Jessica to encourage her to stand strong—while they both fight for the lives that each have built with their spouses and children. But I have to remember that the details of our lives distinguish us from one another, making our situations completely different, yet exactly the same with only our footprints to discern us.

The roles I have assumed in my life were some of my own choosing, some that were thrust upon me, and some that chose me. I spent years trying to live up to society's expectations while casting away its judgments. Is that even possible? I thought so, and I tried. I walked along a backward path in the eyes of confused perception, but my punishment was my own for not fighting harder for me when circumstances were beyond my control. I asked, I waited, and I screamed in silence.

Regret has never had a place in my life, as my children and my husband have always been and will always be the greatest loves of my life. The problem was that I forgot, or maybe never even learned, that I was worthy of my own love and sacrifice. I didn't have to allow anyone else's preconceived notions to taint my worthiness, and I was certainly deserving of my own dreams.

The universe laid out the groundwork one moon after the other for what I needed to do—one post at a time, one beam at a time, from dwelling to dwelling, from camp cottage to our hearts' home, from Floyd's hands into mine. Before I would be truly ready to capture my brightest stars, I needed the force of a mountain to accept with compassion, yield with care, and rise up to meet my destiny with courage.

What did I learn in all of this? I learned that love is the glue that binds us together. I learned that it is okay to set a new standard and create a few of my own rules to follow. I learned that I am allowed to forgive myself for not being the image of perfection that some sought. Most of all, I learned how to look into the mirror and really see who is looking back at me. I am a woman who nurtures from the deepest part of my soul, and a vessel of creativity that travels through my boundless spirit.

And yes, I am a daughter, a sister, a mother, a wife, a student, a medical assistant, a massage therapist, a friend, and a teacher of life. But most of all, I am *Julie*—a woman of endless endurance, infinite hope, and unconditional love, living in harmony with the universe. It's nice to finally meet you.

A letter from my dad:

October 17, 2016

Dear Julie,

As your birthday approaches once more, I want to take time to recognize you for some of the things you are doing. Ten days ago, you drove with Mom to Dana Farber in Boston for her appointment around her annual cancer follow-up. Floyd and you spent Saturday morning watching your grandsons playing football. These are just a few examples of you openly sharing your life with those around you, who you care for, and who care for you …

Those sharing choices have not come without study and discipline on your part. You have taken the time and made the effort to decide how best to share yourself and to assist others in growing wiser in their ways. You have drawn on wisdom from many sources as well as your own experiences. In so doing, you have woven a network of relationships, which in turn have improved the world around you.

In all this, I have admired your diligence and your perseverance. You have grown beyond your years, and you have left your mark in many ways. I am ever so pleased to spend time with you and to watch you in action.

I am ever so proud of you, and I love you for who you are, now and always!

Love,
Dad

About the Author

Julie Brown is a licensed massage therapist and Energy Healer. She has many years of experience in the medical field as both an EMT and Medical Assistant. She has worked as a volunteer massage therapist on the cancer unit at her local hospital and as a mentor teaching infant massage to teen mothers. Julie is the mother of two and grandmother of four. She is passionate about sharing her knowledge about wellness, stress reduction and nutrition.